LIVING
WITH A
DEAD
LANGUAGE

LIVING
WITH A
DEAD
LANGUAGE

MY ROMANCE
WITH LATIN

ANN PATTY

VIKING

VIKING

An imprint of Penguin Random House LLC

375 Hudson Street

New York, New York 10014

penguin.com

Excerpt from "somewhere i have never travelled, gladly beyond" from *Complete Poems: 1904–1962* by E. E. Cummings, edited by George J. Firmage. Copyright 1931, © 1959, 1991 by the Trustees for the E. E. Cummings Trust. Used by permission of Liveright Publishing Corporation.

"That it will never come again" from *The Poems of Emily Dickinson: Variorum Edition,* edited by Ralph W. Franklin, Cambridge, Mass.: The Belknap Press of Harvard University Press. Copyright © 1998 by the President and Fellows of Harvard College. Copyright © 1951, 1955 by the President and Fellows of Harvard College. Copyright © renewed 1979, 1983 by the President and Fellows of Harvard College. Copyright © 1914, 1918, 1919, 1924, 1929, 1930, 1932, 1935, 1937, 1942 by Martha Dickinson Bianchi. Copyright © 1952, 1957, 1958, 1963, 1965 by Mary L. Hampson.

Excerpts from "Burnt Norton" and "East Coker" from *Four Quartets* by T. S. Eliot. Copyright 1936 by Houghton Mifflin Harcourt Publishing Company; copyright © renewed 1964 by T. S. Eliot. Copyright 1940 by T. S. Eliot; copyright © renewed 1968 by Esme Valerie Eliot. Reprinted by permission of Houghton Mifflin Harcourt Publishing Company. All rights reserved.

Plaque from a tomb erected by the soldier Aurelius Achilles for his young son Valentinus; Roman, third century; marble. Columbarium plaque for the freedman Gaius Nonius Salvius; Roman, first-early third century; marble. Frances Lehman Loeb Art Center, Vassar College, Poughkeepsie, New York.

Drawings on pages 30 and 95 by Bernard Greenwald

ISBN 9781101980224 (hardcover)

ISBN 9781101980248 (e-book)

Printed in the United States of America

1   3   5   7   9   10   8   6   4   2

Set in ITC Galliard and Trajan

Designed by Nancy Resnick

For my brother, David Terence Crowder

AUTHOR'S NOTE

All translations from the Latin were done by me. I have not tried to render the Latin into poetic English. While my translations do not demonstrate the beauty of the Latin, they are, as much as I was able, faithful to the literal meanings.

After five years of study, I am at best an amateur Latinist. Any errors of scholarship are mine alone and should not be attributed to my teachers.

ARGUMENTUM

What was to be the value of the long looked forward to,
Long hoped for calm, the autumnal serenity
And the wisdom of age? . . .
The serenity only a deliberate hebetude,
The wisdom only the knowledge of dead secrets

—T. S. Eliot, "East Coker"

"Why on earth would you want to learn Latin at your age?" incredulous friends ask.

I have a short answer and a longer answer. The short answer is because I love words and grammar. The longer answer is, I hope, more interesting and is why I wrote this book.

Hebetude, in the stanza above, comes from the Latin *hebetudo*, from the verb *hebeo*, meaning "to be dull, sluggish, inactive." The *American Heritage Dictionary*, my lexicographic bible for this book, defines hebetude as dullness of mind, mental lethargy.

For thirty-five years, I'd been driven, constantly challenged, not only by my work as a New York editor and publisher, but also by class, competition, men, sex, motherhood, illness, and loss; by everything that is life in New York City.

At fifty-eight, I stopped working and retreated to the

well-earned "autumnal serenity" of my country house in upstate New York. But I was not serene. I was filled with anxiety. What was I to do with myself? How was I to fill the days, the weeks, the months, the years? I was lost in the woods.

My mother was the same age, fifty-eight, when the last of my siblings moved away from home, and I had watched this once industrious, gregarious, lively woman sink into depression, drink, and a feeling of uselessness. She'd lost her metier of running a family of six, and she hadn't the energy to pursue another. "I'm done," she'd say, again and again. I believe she willed herself to die at age sixty-six.

Why did I take up Latin at this late age? I did so not only to fight off hebetude but also to avoid becoming my mother. I had no idea, when I began my studies, that rather than dead secrets, I would discover vital constructs that would illuminate my past as well as my present, and enliven my future. That I would conjure the dead language of my mother to life.

LIVING
WITH A
DEAD
LANGUAGE

CHAPTER 1

Rem tene, verba sequentur.

Grasp the topic, the words will follow.

—Cato the Elder

Verba tene, res sequentur.

Grasp the words, the topic will follow.

—Umberto Eco

It began with benevolence. I was in the seventh grade and my oldest brother, Terry, was home for Thanksgiving. He was in his freshman year in college at UC Berkeley, a short fifteen miles away on the map, but worlds distant from our home on Elysian Fields Drive in East Oakland. Along with such exotica as sautéed mushrooms, espresso coffee, and romaine lettuce, Terry brought home books and words. I don't remember the context in which he used benevolence, but I don't think I had ever heard such a sonorous four-syllable word used in speech before. I wanted that word, and ran off to my room to write it down and look up its meaning in the dictionary. I loved how it extended the concept of kindness into a worldview.

I began collecting words. By ninth grade, I was using my new

I

words in conversation whenever I could. This did not delight my classmates, and forced me to drop the phony stupid-girl act I had adopted in a futile quest for popularity. (In the midsixties, it was the height of uncool at my school to be smart. I still remember being mortified when a friend in eighth grade started telling everyone I got straight A's on my report card.) I decided to become an intellectual, an important-sounding, polysyllabic concept.

Books and words were in short supply in our household. Neither of my parents had gone to college, though my mother was an avid worker of crossword puzzles and often bragged that she was so good at them because she'd studied Latin all during her Catholic education. She'd even won the Latin medal when she graduated from high school. Latin, for her, was the expression of her intelligence. But her engagement with words was solitary, and she did not use Latin words or phrases around us, nor explain how they helped her solve the crossword clues.

The only interest my father showed in words was in trying to rid us of certain verbal tics that annoyed him: Whenever one of us (too frequently) said, "Ya'know?" he would say, "No, I don't know." Whenever we said, "That's true," he would say, "No. True lives across the street." True being the name of the doctor's wife in the pink ranch opposite our house.

After benevolence, I was always on the alert for new words that came my way, and I'd add them to my growing list of words and their definitions. I'd test myself against the "It Pays to Enrich Your Word Power" pages in the monthly *Reader's Digest*. Soon I knew all the words on offer there.

During high school I spent most of my spare time reading, writing bad poetry, and discussing books (often recommended by Terry) with my best friend, Shannon. Words had become my other best friend: I spent hours following strings of synonyms through the dictionary. I became obsessed with suffixes, especially with words ending in -id. I loved the -id words: languid, pellucid, insipid, intrepid. They have an interior, intense quality; the -id ending carries the scent of moral or esthetic indulgence, whether good or bad. It forces the tongue to execute a dental stop to finish the word, as if it's entitled. Even before I knew Freud's id, and what it meant, I seemed to have intuited it in many -id words. Each seemed a quiddity (!) of a state of being, complete in itself. After several years, my collection of -id words was large enough to construct the House of Ids.

```
                        acid
             acrid            actinoid
          arid                  arachnid
       bifid         candid       carotid
       felid                      fervid
       fetid                      flaccid
       florid                     fluid
       frigid                     gravid
       horrid                     humid
       insipid                    intrepid
       irid                       limpid
       liquid                     livid
       lucid                      morbid
       pallid                     pavid
       pellucid                   perfervid
       placid                     putrid
       rancid                     rigid
       sapid                      solid
       sordid                     splendid
       squalid                    staid
       timid                      valid
       vapid          void        viscid
```

The house above is not the original house, but one that has continued to expand over the years, with each new -id addition. I've gone as long as seven years between new -ids, but inevitably, much to my delight, I encounter a new one. At one point, I had to make rules: adjectives only (thus excluding the lovely noun caryatid and the exciting verbid); no scientific/chemical/geometric terms such as ootid, nitid, ovoid, and rhomboid. Since void was not only an adjective but also a noun and a verb, it was given pride of place—the central base of the house. The word walls protected me from the void, which, even when I was young, seemed to yap at my heels. I built words around it.

Soon after I built the first House of Ids, I began constructing walls of -itys, -iles, -ines, and -asms, but those lists led nowhere compelling: It was becoming too big a collection, a word neighborhood organized by suffix, perhaps not the most useful of endeavors.

Most, if not all, -id adjectives have cousin nouns ending in -or, though some had no remaining noun in usage (What is morbor? Or frigor? Or putror?). In fact, I later learned, many come from Latin adjectives ending in -*idus* (*morbidus, frigidus, putridus*) with the -*us* dropped. They were Latinate, to be sure, but as I had never learned Latin, I didn't really know what Latinate meant. Dictionaries defined it as "a style derived from Latin," but that was unhelpful. Without knowing Latin, how could I know its style?

At my public junior high in Oakland, we were required to take a semester of Latin in the seventh grade; the second semester the girls were rewarded with homemaking (where we learned to make cotton aprons, bacon-and-cheese rollups, and three-layer gelatin salad) and the boys with woodshop (where they learned to make boxes and leaf-shaped trivets).

Latin class was held in a "portable"—a beige wooden trailer of a classroom, one of several that stood in a double row at the back of the school, housing the overflow of the baby boom. The room was dark, stuffy, and usually overheated. Our teacher, Mr. Abayta, was Basque, a small, dark man, always formally dressed in a well-worn suit and tie. Not a typical Californian, he was known throughout the school for having bad breath, and each semester some rascally student or another would leave a large bottle of mouthwash on his desk. He was considered the weirdest, most boring teacher in the school, which I understand now was because of the combination of his old-world, dowdy appearance, his coming from a region that none of us had ever heard of, and his subject: Latin.

The only thing I remember learning in that class was the first declension:

agricola	*agricolae*
agricolae	*agricolarum*
agricolae	*agricolis*
agricolam	*agricolas*
agricola	*agricolis*

The class was rowdy and unengaged, and our tests were laughably easy. One consisted of the above written on the blackboard, and a new root word, *puella,* written on the test sheet, so we merely had to add the endings to the new root word. In other words, all you had to do was memorize the suffixes. Perhaps that is what had started me on the House of Ids.

I'm sure I inherited my lifelong love of reading from my Indiana grandfather, Elias. He had read Latin—he even had some Latin books in his library, consisting of six glass-fronted bookshelves in the "music room," which also held my grandmother's piano, long unused due to her arthritis. It was a dark room, with tattered green blinds always closed, musty with the smell, I would later recognize, of old clothbound books. I slept on a cot there when we visited.

Elias was a tall, slender, taciturn man with a full head of upright white hair, turquoise eyes, and one gold-rimmed front tooth. He was startlingly handsome, but cold. He was well respected in his tiny Indiana town, held an MA degree from Marion University, and had been a schoolteacher for a few years before he became the youngest councilman of the town and, soon after, a banker. "He once brought someone to give a talk at the town hall," my dad told me, "and no one but Elias had any idea what the man was talking about." My father did not get along with Elias. He found his father's learned pursuits to be a waste of time. My father was focused on earning money. Though extremely bright, he seemed to have no interest in the life of the mind.

I saw little of Elias on our summer visits. Every night he'd come home from his job at the bank, change into his farm clothes, and go out behind the barn to spend time with his hogs before dinner. He still favored the outhouse over the indoor bathroom, and washed at the slop sink in the mudroom rather than in the bathroom of the house. After dinner, he'd retire to his Lloyd Loom chair in the living room and read while the rest of us watched the tiny ovoid television in the corner.

I remember only one conversation with him. It was about books. I was fifteen, lying on the high and uncomfortable

"Indian" horsehair couch next to Grandpa's chair. We were both reading. I was totally absorbed in *The Gallery* by John Horne Burns, which Terry had passed on to me. It consisted of linked stories about an American GI experiencing louche post-war Naples—the Galleria he frequented comprised bars, brothels, and not a few homosexuals, an entirely new concept to me. I was riveted. After a while, Elias put down his own book and asked if he could have a look at mine. It didn't take him long to scan a few pages and pronounce the book trash. He was aghast at the language and subject matter. He told me I should not read such books, and went on to recommend I seek morally uplifting literature, such as *Quo Vadis,* and anything by Booth Tarkington. He then returned to his own book.

Many years later, I finally read *Quo Vadis.* And it is indeed a moral tale dramatizing the powerful lure of the Christian spirit in decadent Rome. A fierce warrior falls obsessively in love with a young Christian woman, and finally follows her god as the way into her pants, at least from my cynical reading. That book was among the regrettably few I took from my grandfather's effects after he died: I did not take his small Latin text of *The Aeneid* (an id!). I could not then imagine I'd ever read it. I did take three novels by Booth Tarkington, *A Hoosier Chronicle* by Meredith Nicholson, and a couple of old texts on personal hygiene. *The People's Common Sense Medical Adviser* warned against the sin of onanism, which might lead to dereliction, madness, drug abuse, and premature death. It didn't say anything about logophilia.

I was pleasantly surprised, when I finally read *Alice Adams* and *The Magnificent Ambersons,* to see what a fine writer Booth Tarkington was: a sharp, sophisticated chronicler of class, a bit of Edith Wharton in the Midwest. My grandfather had surprised me, thirty years after his death.

Through my studies in comparative literature at UC Berkeley, I became fluent in French and discovered how the study of a foreign language increased one's understanding of the grammar, syntax, and worldview of one's native tongue—not to mention ramping up one's interest in etymology. Just before I graduated, I met two women at a party in Sausalito who were book editors in New York. The clichéd lightbulb illuminated above my head. I should move to New York and get a job editing books. That's what I knew and loved: books and language, my lifelines out of boredom and emptiness.

I decided to follow those lifelines to Manhattan, where I found a job in paperback publishing. After a few driven years, I had worked my way up from starving editorial assistant to associate editor to senior editor. By the time I was twenty-seven years old, I had discovered V. C. Andrews, one of the most successful paperback writers of the 1980s, as well as a string of other best sellers. I parlayed that success into a hardcover imprint, the Poseidon Press, which allowed me to publish both commercial and literary titles.

In my early New York years, I still kept company with the majority of American English speakers who confound the verbs to lay and to lie, and don't distinguish less from fewer, or the objective from the nominative case (e.g., the all-too-common, ear-offending "between you and I").

My first husband, a midwestern aristo who was educated at private schools and Yale, shamed those misuses out of me. He was, as my mother perspicaciously declared, my graduate school. After I'd mastered usage, like most autodidacts I took up the cause of the Grammar Police, often to the point of obnoxiousness.

Words were my way to becoming who I wanted to be, both in my own mind and in the world. I read those classics not included in my education and continued to hone my grammar and syntactical skills. Whenever I came across a word I didn't know, I looked it up and added it to the word lists I still kept in the back of my journals. After ten years in publishing, I seldom ran across a word I didn't know, but I was always glad when I did, especially when it was *le mot juste*.

My publishing career ended thirty-four years later, at the dawn of the recession of 2008. For the previous seven years, I'd had the perfect situation: I worked part-time, edited only five or six titles a year. I was more successful than ever, acquiring and editing *Life of Pi*, *A Three Dog Life*, *The Crimson Petal and the White*, among other critically acclaimed best sellers. No matter. The recession was disastrous for the already highly leveraged company. I was among forty to be laid off in a single day.

Luckily, I'd unconsciously set myself up for an early retirement. In 2006, the year my daughter left for college, I had sold my apartment in New York and used the spoils to rebuild my weekend house in rural Rhinebeck in upstate New York. Like every book editor, I had spent many hours reading and editing at home, but now I spent more of those hours in the country. I could put on my telephone earpiece and have editorial discussions while pulling weeds in my garden. I stayed in the city two or three nights a week, where I could still enjoy the conversations, lunches, dinners, and parties that were the social side benefit of my professional life, but I had the peace and quiet of the country to come home to.

During the first winter, however, living in the country began to seem like a foolhardy, even disastrous, decision. Was it possible to find happiness in the middle of eleven rural acres with only my dog, Augie, a twelve-pound poodle, for company? There were no other houses or people visible from my property, only a few winter birds, and the surrounding silence of the brown and grey woods.

That spring, I hazarded Match.com, mostly to prove to myself that I would never meet an appropriate man in the country, that I should give up and sell my newly rebuilt house, admit a (quite costly) mistake, and move back to Manhattan. My property was too much, too isolated for a woman alone. And really, I was a city girl.

I typed in my zip code and the first man to pop up was George, the cute fellow I had noticed in the one Iyengar yoga class offered in my town. I'd wanted to get next to him for quite a while, but I always arrived early, he late (a duet at which we became adept). His nom de Match was Aquila, Latin for Eagle. I liked the Latin and I liked his profile. My nom de Match was Jakuan. A Zen student himself, George recognized Jakuan as a dharma name and looked up the meaning: Serenity.

Like all Match.com ads, ours were both guilty of false advertising, if only by inference. George didn't know Latin, he wasn't well read, and he had a tin ear for language. And I was anything but serene.

Nevertheless, we fell in love. He stayed one night and never left.

That was either great good fortune or a great irony of fate or both. Eight months later I was fired. Moving back to New York was out of the question, both financially and romantically. George was a quintessential country man.

My rural domain had been a perfect counterpoint to the hurly-burly of New York City. But when I lost my job and the literary community that had sustained me for over thirty years, it felt like exile. The e-mails and phone calls that used to engage a few hours every day ceased to arrive. Now I spent my days reading, preparing meals, gardening, walking with my dog along quiet country lanes, organizing cabinets, making all those household perfections I'd never had time for, and that, frankly, I didn't care much about. And then what?

I never could have imagined, when I was an overly busy New York editor and exhausted single mother, that there could be too much time, that an abundance of free time could become a source of dread. The days meandered into one another, weekdays indistinguishable from weekends, mornings, afternoons, evenings, whole days of dawdling. I had lost my identity. I had lost my purpose, which had been driving me so hard for so long that I hadn't realized its power. I'd even lost the purpose of earning a living. I wasn't rich, but I had pensions and savings and I could bring in some extra income with freelance work. And living in the country was so much cheaper than in the city. I was fifty-eight years old and hoped for twenty or even thirty more years *compos mentis*. That was almost as many years as I'd been an editor in the large New York publishing world. How would I fill so many days, months, years? Who was I now, without the work that had been my passionate purpose and my goad for thirty-four years? The exterior compulsions were gone but I was still here. What was I going to do with my still driven, anxious self, ever closer to the void yawning before me?

Maybe I should find some way to enact my desire to make the study of grammar and syntax popular and fun. Perhaps I should write a children's book and build a proper sentence, adding one part of speech per page in some really clever way. I even came up with the first page:

LOOK!

A perfectly acceptable sentence, an imperative verb, but lonely, without even a named subject

That was as far as I got. I was in the same situation as the sentence—lonely and in need of a subject.

I always used to tell young people who didn't know what to do with their lives, "Pick something you're interested in, invest some time in it, and if it clicks, that something will inevitably lead you somewhere, a job, a hobby, a passion." I pondered what I had enjoyed most, and the answer kept coming up: words, grammar, books, language. I had worked in that world my entire adult life. What had I missed?

I had missed Latin. I had missed knowing the roots of my word home. How much better would I understand words, grammar, and syntax if I went back to the mother of Western tongues? I could, at long last, complete my education. I could, after all these years, learn what Latinate actually meant. I could, *ex post facto,* share a language with my mother. And a classroom would put me in the company of young people, give me a reason to get out of my pajamas, take a bath, and leave the house. I researched the colleges in my area and was dismayed to learn that none of the three community colleges or two nearby state colleges offered Latin. Not even the Catholic college offered it. How had this subject, once essential for any educated person, dropped so completely from the syllabus?

Finally, to my great relief, I discovered that Bard College, a small, private liberal arts college near me, did offer Latin. I sent an e-mail plea to the professor who would be teaching the beginning course in September, asking him to let me audit. My Web site was below my signature; I had discovered well-known and important writers. It was clear I was a serious literary person. I assumed he'd welcome me. Wouldn't I be a good influence on the youngsters in class—an old person taking Latin for no reason but love? He wrote back, "I'm sorry to say but I have a policy never to let anyone audit a first-year language course. I find it never works." He went on to add that I was welcome to officially enroll in the course. I phoned the registrar: The fee would be $5,600 a semester.

That set me back for a year, another year of wondering how I'd possibly survive another twenty (or, a scary thought, thirty) years without becoming a drunk, a bore, a depressive. I had watched my mother live that death-in-life trio for the last ten years of her life. If I followed her path, I'd be dead in eight years.

So I took on more and more uninspiring freelance work and honed my gourmet cooking skills. With the companion-ship of too many glasses of wine, I could while away hours comparing recipes, shopping, and preparing meals, which delighted George. I gained ten pounds. Most of my hours were spent reading. I explored the wonders and limitations of the Kindle: I could sample the first chapter of a book before I bought it, thus saving myself buying well-reviewed but not-to-my-taste novels. I had spent so many years wading through manuscripts, searching for something engaging, so many years having so little "antidotal" reading time, that my reading tastes were now more stringent than ever. The five volumes of Trollope's Palliser novels were great on the Kindle and kept me occupied for a few weeks. (From him I learned the delightful word "quidnunc," meaning a nosy person, from the Latin mean-ing, literally, what now?) The essays of David Foster Wallace, with so many footnotes, so many Latin words, and so many abbreviations that I was familiar with but didn't truly know the meaning of, required a printed book. What is the differ-ence between *cf.* and *viz.* and *q.v.*? And what exactly did *QED* mean? I didn't know. I looked it up in the *American Heritage Dictionary.* "QED: *abbr. Latin* quod erat demonstrandum (which was to be demonstrated)." I would later learn that the construction is called a passive periphrastic by Latinists, and is more perfectly translated expressing necessity: "which was needing to be demonstrated." There it was. My need had been demonstrated.

The following summer I researched Latin classes at Vassar College in Poughkeepsie. A year ago it had seemed too distant, a forty-five-minute drive away. I hated the endless driving country living required. All those years in New York City had accustomed me to walking and public transportation. Lone car driving seemed irresponsible: all that fuel for only one person. Nevertheless, the destination would be worthy. The yearlong course met four days a week at 9:00 A.M. That would certainly fill up a few hours of my empty life.

I googled Curtis Dozier, the professor who would be teaching beginning Latin. On the Rate Your Professor Web site I found these comments:

He's quirky and nerdy, but in the best possible way and you can really tell that he's passionate about Latin. Plus he's cute.

He geeks out all the time. He's very invested in teaching—he cried the last day of class—most adorable thing EVER.

I e-mailed Curtis Dozier and arranged to meet him at his office a month before class was to begin. He was a skinny, strawberry blond, Herman's Hermits–type man (my major seventh-grade crush), only three years older than my daughter, shy, serious, and definitely adorable. He had gotten his PhD from UC Berkeley, my alma mater, only two years before, and he was used to having auditors in his classes. He was a great fan of *Life of Pi,* so was happy to have me in his class. I was worried that I would have trouble with all the memorization, but he thought my background in French would help me considerably.

"Why do you want to do this?" he asked. "It's a lot of work."

"I love words," I told him. "And now I don't work anymore, and I'm sort of going crazy and I really need to keep my brain, and thus myself, alive, and I really need some outside structure and . . ." He stopped my rush of words with an upraised hand and a smile. "I understand completely," he said. As I was leaving, thanking him, calling him Professor Dozier, he said, "And you can call me Curtis."

I was *in*! I would be a Vassar girl. In high school, when I'd read *The Group,* Mary McCarthy's privileged, sophisticated Vassar girls seemed to inhabit a world light-years from mine. I'd known a number of women and men—the college had gone coed in 1974—who had attended Vassar, but I'd never visited the campus. And what a beautiful campus it is: traditionally Ivy League (or Seven Sisters in this case) with imposing ivy-covered Collegiate Gothic buildings, as well as some modern additions, which give it both a contemporary and classical feel. Not much was going on that summer day, but it was a lovely place to walk: winding pathways snaking among architecturally pleasing buildings, with well-maintained landscaping and sprawling specimen trees gracing the many lawns.

I arrived at 8:00 A.M. for the first day of class, a hot, sunny, late August day. Class didn't start for an hour, but I needed to buy the textbook and I wanted to appear serious and prepared. The bookstore shelves, alphabetically keyed to classes, went from

Chinese to Computer Science: no Classics section. When I asked at the desk, I was told Classics had been renamed "Greek and Roman Studies," GRST for short. Its four shelves of offerings were between the larger domains of German Studies and Hispanic Studies. I later learned that Classics had been changed to GRST only the year before; a young woman was the department chair, and she had convinced her colleagues that the term "classics" was outmoded and implied a value judgment. Who were they to appropriate the term "classic" only to their field of study? Political correctness was alive and well at Vassar. Besides, she thought Greek and Roman Studies sounded more appealing, likely to attract more students. The text and accompanying workbook, *Learn to Read Latin,* were expensive, ninety dollars, and must have weighed eight pounds.

Our class was held in the Sanders Classroom, a three-story, redbrick, copper-roofed building in the Georgian style. It was decidedly less elegant inside than out. Latin met on the first floor, half below grade, in a large corner room. I was the first to arrive. Thirty student desks of varying style and vintage, some wood, most plastic, were haphazardly scattered around the room, and a metal teacher's desk angled before the freshly washed blackboard that spanned the wall at the front of the room. I hadn't been in such a room for close to forty years, but I recognized the smell immediately: chalk dust and books and anticipation, the smells of learning. I figured that as an auditor I should sit at the back, so I positioned myself in the last row on the eastern side of the room. Along with my new books, I had bought a spiral notebook, puce, with pockets inside for loose papers.

Around 8:45 the students began dribbling in. Most of them looked like freshmen, but a few weren't. I could tell by the way they walked, whether they recognized another classmate, how they chose their desk. Three cute gay boys, jolly and talkative, sat together along the east wall next to the door. A tall, lumpy fellow galumphed in, then others, mostly singly, one boy-girl pair. No new arrival chose to sit closer than two desks away from me, a lone grey head in a sea of fresh-faced youth. Finally, an eccentrically dressed brunette sat next to me. I was so relieved! The young woman's name was Camilla. She was a freshman from Idaho. An art major, she loved literature and so had decided to learn Latin. Her mother was a single, hard-working nurse, and Camilla had a campus job. She was also on the golf team. Of course I learned all this later, after she'd become my best friend in class. Another girl, overweight, truculent Stella, sat next to Camilla.

There was not a piercing or tattoo to be seen among the students. Only one thin young man, who suffered some sort of ambulatory awkwardness, had a magenta stripe running from forehead to nape through his hair; another, with the looks and carriage of a heartbreaker, sported a soul patch. Out of twenty-one there was one Hispanic student, one black, fourteen males, and seven females. That was a surprise, since Vassar had far more women than men, and literary fields usually attracted many more females than males. I would learn, as the year progressed, how much Rome, with its emphasis on power, war, and building, was a male domain, and thus attracted its own.

On that first day, as on every day thereafter, Curtis Dozier arrived at exactly 9:00. "*Salvete discipuli!*" He pronounced it as he wrote it on the board; he then declaimed and wrote our response: "*Salve Magister!*" We repeated in unison. At first strike, it was a perfect distillation of the preeminence of hierarchy in ancient Rome, passed down now in English: master and disciple.

17

Curtis passed out index cards, on which we were to write how much Latin we'd studied previously and why we were taking the class. When I later interviewed several of the students, I discovered that most of them had already had a few years of Latin in high school. An alarming number of them, including some of the best Latinists, were taking the class because it was the only language class that didn't meet on Fridays. All the other foreign language classes met five days a week, at 9:00 A.M., and a full year's language study was a graduation requirement at Vassar. So much for seriousness! A day a week's extra sleep was worth the drudgey eccentricity of Latin.

One young man who, it became obvious as the year progressed, was the worst in the class, was being forced to take Latin by his father. Roger was an economics student and had no interest in language. But his father prided himself on his proficiency in Latin, and made Roger's Latin studies a financial requirement. My father had done the same thing to me, only from the opposite discipline, when he had forced me to take an economics class at Berkeley so I would "learn something useful" for his investment. I had been infuriated by his wasting my time with that class, though as the years passed I became more and more grateful: It had helped me understand the flow of money in the world. When I had first wrangled my own imprint at Simon and Schuster, the CFO said to a colleague, "It's nice Ann got an imprint; she's the only editor who ever comes to me to discuss the finances of books. And she's made a lot of money for the company. The only thing that worries me is that she has a *literary* bent." (*Pax, Pater.*)

Economics and literature might intersect in business and academia, but clearly the intent of each inhabits a world foreign to the other.

Curtis spent the rest of the forty-five-minute class period

covering administrative details: He reminded everyone that it was a full-year class, and no credit would be given if you dropped out between semesters. There would be a quiz every Thursday, as well as a midterm and a final, and homework every night. He then introduced Ella, the senior student assistant, who would hold review sessions and be available for one-on-one tutoring: He encouraged us to use her; she had been awarded the hours, and she needed to earn them. She was the opposite of what I might have expected, a sultry, exotic beauty, sexily dressed, and with a rippling mane of black hair. With that, Curtis bade us *Salvete*.

CHAPTER 2

The principles and rules of grammar are the means by which the forms of language are made to correspond with the universal forms of thought. The distinctions between the various parts of speech, between the cases of nouns, the moods and tenses of verbs, the functions of participles, are distinctions in thought, not merely in words.

—John Stuart Mill

The next morning, I awoke with the sun, and rather than lolling abed, as was my habit, I thought I'd be a good classical scholar and live by that celestial body, as the Romans did. I was so excited I didn't even bathe, but dressed and got in my car, tea in hand, and drove to campus, even though I knew I'd be almost two hours early for class. I was used to arriving early for things. I even had to wait thirty minutes to check out the breakfast offerings at "The Retreat," which didn't open until 7:30. It wasn't the official cafeteria, but more of a large snack bar in the main building. I was early even there—only the slim, slope-backed janitor, with whom I would develop a friendly acquaintance over the next four years, was there finishing up his mopping. Since I was starting a new era, one fixed by morning discipline and study, I avoided the delicious-looking blueberry muffins and cranberry-walnut scones and dished myself up a small bowl of oatmeal. Condiments of raisins, blueberries, granola, and brown sugar were offered. I eschewed only the brown sugar.

At this opening hour, there was only one other patron in the entire Retreat. I sat at a sunny table near the window and paged through *Learn to Read Latin*. It had fifteen chapters, all of which we would cover over the course of the next nine months. Each chapter began with a list of forty or so vocabulary words. And what should be the very first word of the very first vocabulary list of Chapter I but *agricola*—the only Latin word I remembered from that lone seventh-grade semester. Obviously, some things never change. Food, and those who provide it, always comes first.

At 8:45 I headed to class. Again I was the first to arrive. I had to rearrange the scattered mess of desks to sit in the back row on the eastern side, as I had the day before. When she finally arrived, Camilla again sat next to me, and Stella next to her. Week in and week out almost all the students sat in the same place in relation to those around them, even though the desks needed organizing every morning. Only one student, a young woman whom I came to call Insouciant Inez, traveled around the western regions of the *patria* (a first-declension noun meaning homeland, included in the vocabulary list on page one of Chapter I). She would sit here or there with a careless slouch and an air of indulgent superiority, her feet usually resting on an empty desk she'd stationed in front of hers. I later learned she was a senior, well versed in Latin, who was taking this class for an easy A.

A few students engaged with their smartphones while waiting for Curtis to arrive, but most paged through their textbooks.

Curtis arrived at 9:00 on the dot, greeted us with *Salvete*, turned on the lights, and took up his position behind the desk.

Every day the class sat in the penumbra awaiting his arrival, until finally, about a month into the semester, he said, "You know, I've noticed that the only class I teach in which no one turns on the lights is nine A.M. Latin. Why do you suppose that is?" After that, I turned on the lights if I was the first to arrive; others followed suit. The following year the college decided there would be no more 9:00 A.M. classes; the earliest class would begin at 9:30.

That first week we were introduced, both in our textbooks and by Curtis, to "The Latin Noun and Its Properties: Gender, Number, Case." Gender and number I had practiced with both English and French (though Latin added neuter to masculine and feminine), but not case. Case means inflection: Each word has a suffix that fixes its role in the sentence as subject, direct or indirect object, or adverbial object. In the Latin sentence, words can appear in any order the writer wishes, so the only way to "read" and thus comprehend the sentence is to "read" the suffixes and thus discern what part the word plays in the sentence. For example:

Poeta puellam amat means "The poet loves the girl," as does *Puellam poeta amat;* but *Poetam puella amat* and *Puella poetam amat* mean "The girl loves the poet."

Here I was again, with my beloved suffixes, beginning with endings. The -ids I'd begun collecting all those years ago could loosely be called an inflection that renders a noun an adjective in English—horror: horrid; torpor: torpid.

Wikipedia provides a daunting summary of case and inflection:

> Latin, the mother tongue of the Romance languages, was highly inflected; nouns and adjectives had different forms according to seven grammatical cases (including five major ones) with five major patterns of

declension, and three genders instead of the two found in most Romance tongues. There were four patterns of conjugation in six tenses, three moods (indicative, subjunctive, imperative, plus the infinitive, participle, gerund, gerundive, and supine) and two voices (passive and active), all overtly expressed by affixes (passive voice forms were periphrastic in three tenses).

QED: The head spins. This is what I'd signed up for.

On that second day, after his *Salvete,* Curtis called roll using the cards he'd collected the day before. I awaited my name to be called with some exhilaration: When had I last been in a roll call? I was a member of a class. On my card I'd written, "No previous Latin," and "Passionate desire." I hoped that pleased him. I was eager to please him.

For the next week Curtis would use the cards to call on us during class and to learn our names. If no one answered to a card, he would toss it aside. You were allowed only five absences before your grade was affected. I decided I'd follow that rule and never miss a class out of laziness. I'd had quite enough laziness in the past two years; this was a necessary and welcome daily dose of discipline and engagement.

That morning we were introduced to the first declension (nouns ending in *a* in the nominative case). A declension is a way of grouping nouns that follow a similar pattern of inflection. In Latin, inflection (from *inflecto, inflectere,* to bend or change) doesn't have the many associations it has in English: It refers only to the suffix (inflection) added to the noun's root to establish its syntax (which part of speech the noun plays in a sentence). Unlike English, in which the placement of the noun determines its role in the sentence, in Latin, it is the inflection, or ending, that determines the role a noun plays in the sentence. There are five different declensions (different patterns of endings) for nouns. Nouns are always cited in both their nominative and genitive cases (*puella, puellae*), because the genitive signals which of the five declensions govern the noun.

The first declension is the first taught in nearly every Latin text. Most first declension nouns are feminine—queen (*regina*), woman (*femina*), goddess (*dea*), girl (*puella*). Only a few masculine nouns—poet (*poeta*), farmer (*agricola*), and sailor (*nauta*)—are included in this declension.

A mnemonic from long ago tries to explain:

> All nouns in *a* make Feminine,
> If you like "Musa" them decline,
> Except they're from a Graecian line,
> Or by their sense are Masculine.

Does this help? What if you don't know Greek? And why would the "masculine in sense" nouns such as *agricola* (farmer), *nauta* (sailor), *poeta* (poet) be included in a feminine declension? Though Curtis didn't enter that thicket, I tried to penetrate the logic of the language. Was it perhaps because the "masculine in sense" nouns related somehow to taming nature (*natura* also feminine)? Most things having to do with the earth (*terra, provincia*) are first-declension feminine nouns, and certainly *agricola* and *nauta* are intimate with the earth. And life itself (*vita*) is feminine. But what does that say about the Roman view of the poet (*poeta*)? Does the first declension hark back to earlier, preverbal times, before the patriarchy, when the earth goddess ruled and all toil was at her pleasure? *Accola* (neighbor), *advena* (foreigner, stranger), *conlega* (colleague), and *conviva* (guest) are also first-declension masculine nouns. Perhaps because neighbors, strangers, colleagues, and guests, like women, were under the command of men? *Scriba* (secretary, scribe) is understandable as masculine, since few women in those days were literate. No surprise, however, that it's in a feminine declension, since it's a subordinate role. I myself had spent many years on that professional *via* (road, which is feminine), and I remember watching my mother take dictation from my father. She knew shorthand, a now obsolete skill that few, if any, men ever learned. And what about *pecunia* (property, wealth), which is also first-declension feminine? Is it because it is something to be conquered by the second-declension *viri* (men)? *Ecastor!* (By Castor!)

The nominative is the easiest case; it names the subject of the sentence. It's a case familiar to all English speakers. *Nomen=* name. "This is the most straightforward of the cases," Curtis said. It is the nominative noun one tries to find first when translating a Latin sentence. It's not necessarily the first word in a sentence, and it sometimes looks identical to the accusative case, but compared to the other cases, it's not difficult to figure out its role in the sentence. I came to think of it as home base.

The genitive is the possessive case, most often translated as "of." Simple, yes? *Patria puellae* (the country of the girl or the girl's country). Until you realize that it has other functions, increasingly more eccentric. The word genitive comes from *genus* (family, breed, species, tribe, descendant), which links comfortably with English ideas and helps explain the genitive of characteristic and the genitive of description. But how does the genitive of indefinite value fit in there? I had no idea. Even odder, the genitive of the exciting cause. Curtis avoided these complexities in the first week, though they would be doled out, often two at a time, in subsequent weeks.

The dative is the case of the indirect object (to or for). When you know that *datum* is a gift, and *datus* means "having been given," the case becomes clearer. Though not for everyone: Some students, not adept at English grammar, had a lot of trouble with it. Curtis had to call on three students before one could identify the indirect object in the English sentence "I give you a lesson" (you is the dative). This case is a workhorse, with many roles in addition to the indirect object. Luckily, we would not be introduced to the more arcane uses of the dative till much later: the dative of advantage and disadvantage, the dative of the possessor, the dative of purpose, the dative of reference, and the capper, the dative of agent with the passive periphrastic. *Ohe iam!* (Enough already!)

The accusative is the case of the direct object. The root comes from the same root as cause, so it is what is caused by the action of the verb. So in our simple sentence, *Poeta puellam amat, puellam* (girl) is the accusative. Even to this apparently logical case Latin adds complications, which would also be covered in subsequent chapters of our textbook: the accusative of duration of time, the accusative of exclamation, the accusative of place to which, and the accusative of respect.

The latter, a favorite of Latin poets, seems almost purposefully awkward and obfuscating, though I would come to know it well two years later when I began studying the poets. Ovid especially seemed to favor the locution for describing hair. Viz., Ovid *Amores* I.i: "*longas compta puella comas*" (a girl well arranged in respect to her long hair) and Ovid *Amores* III.ix: "*inornatas dilaniata comas*" (mutilated in respect to her disheveled hair), which refers to the practice of mourning common in Rome—women tearing their hair out.

I came of age in publishing in the seventies, the boom time of the paperback romances, whose authors, like Ovid, spent a

26

lot of time describing the conditions of the heroine's hair, although no romance novelist had ever presented hair with the accusative of respect. *She was well arranged in respect to her hair*? I think not. But likely the focus on the romance heroine's hair had come all the way down from Ovid.

The ablative is known as the adverbial case and expresses separation (from), association (with), instrument (by), or location (in, on, or at). An easy example: *Poeta pecuniam de puella aufert.* (The poet carries away money from the girl.) The girl (*puella*) is in the ablative case.

The word ablative comes from the Latin *ablatus,* carried away. And indeed, the case is carried away with its own self: It is by far the largest and most consternating of the cases. Here are the various additional uses of the ablative that we would learn over the year: the ablative of cause, the ablative of comparison, the ablative of degree of difference, the ablative of description, the ablative of manner, the ablative of origin, the ablative of personal agent, the ablative of price, the ablative of respect, the ablative absolute, and the ablative of specification.

Then there is the ablative of attendant circumstances, which even most textbooks leave out. It is what scholars call the use of an ablative in Roman literature that doesn't fit comfortably into any of the other categories of ablative. *Pro di immortales!* (By the immortal gods!)

Even Emily Dickinson, it seems, knew the ablative well, indeed accorded the capacious case estatehood:

That It Will Never Come Again

That it will never come again
Is what makes life so sweet.

27

Believing what we don't believe
Does not exhilarate.
That if it be, it be at best
An ablative estate—
This instigates an appetite
Precisely opposite.

I wonder if she was referring to the ablative of separation. Or the fact that the estate is so large, and greedy: It appropriates any prepositional idea not safely stored in the double garages of the dative and the accusative.

The easy, friendly vocative finished up the cases: It is the case of direct address and has no other agenda waiting in the wings. And, except for the second declension singular, its endings are identical to the nominatives!

Here's a sentence using them all:

Professor, I will give you an egg on Easter. *Pascha tibi, Magister, ovum donabo.* In this sentence the nominative I is contained in the inflection (*o*) of the verb, *donabo.*

Every day, as I drove to Poughkeepsie and back, I practiced the vocabulary given for the first chapter. I hadn't attempted to memorize anything in close to thirty-five years. I had been a Zen student for more than ten years, but I still hadn't committed the entire Heart Sutra to memory, even though I must have chanted it hundreds of times. In learning the vocabulary I was exercising a weak, atrophied muscle, and exercise I did. When I memorized, I could actually feel a spot of awareness and muscle fatigue about an inch above the outside of my left ear. Was that the memory center of my brain? Rather than sing while I drove, I chanted Latin nouns. When I was abed and sleep eluded me, I chased declensions rather than sheep.

After the second week of class, we took our first Thursday quiz. Having spent so many hours memorizing the vocabulary and the first two declensions, I thought I'd aced the test. I'd always been a self-satisfied test taker, the fastest kid in the room. Not this time.

I'd gotten only six out of ten, barely passing. I was not one of the smarties in the class; in fact, I seemed to be one of the dummies.

"Oh, dear, I think this is very bad," I said to Camilla. She continued to sit beside me every day, often in some unlikely outfit, a bit of homey dash and sass. That day she wore a skirt printed with large, bright purple and yellow flowers and a red-and-white-striped T-shirt. We were getting into the habit of chatting before class most days, usually comparing homework or asking advice on some syntax we didn't understand. "How did you do?" I asked her.

She showed me her quiz: eight out of ten. "Well, better than me," I said as I slid mine over to her. "I don't think I've ever done this badly on a test before in my life," I lamented. I actually had that sinking feeling of failure in my stomach. She gave me a look, at once ironic and compassionate, and picked up the pile of cards on her desk. "You need to make flash cards," she advised. "It's the best way to memorize."

After class, I stopped at the bookstore and bought index cards. Which would be better: 3x5 or 2x3? I got two packages of the smaller, two of the larger; white for nouns, blue for verbs, the large ones for syntactical difficulties. Always being a thrifty sort, I did not make them, as Camilla did, one word per card, Latin on one side, English on the other, but rather squashed three words with translations on each card. I left the back blank, figuring I would need it later.

I began taking the cards along on my daily walks with Augie, who was getting on in years but still lively and up for fun. The two hundred acres of hilly farmland across the street, now cultivated into a parklike private domain by my neighbor, were my memorizing fields. On those long walks, I'd let Augie run at will off the leash, as I repeated the words on one card after another. No one was around to hear me, and saying them aloud, again and again, seemed to plant them firmly in my brain. Farm fields nurtured words.

In the third week, prepositions (of which there are fewer in Latin than one might expect—many prepositions are backed into the inflection) were introduced, accompanied by the only drawing in the entire text, a version of which is rendered below:

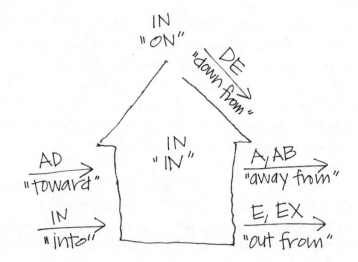

This new word house delighted me. How concise Latin is! The language, like Roman architecture, is sturdy, carefully fitted together, built to withstand the incursions of time. Roman edifices and bridges have weathered millennia, one heavy stone placed next to or atop another, their mortar the architectural equivalent of declensions and conjugations. Everything fits snugly, compactly. That's what gives the language its ponderous feel and its grandeur. Still I loved the drawing of the house, and imagined the prepositions as vermin, climbing in and out of the walls of English and French nouns. They were not unlike the vermin that remained in my house, even after I'd spent a small fortune on its rebuilding.

Learning a language is much like building a new home, or constructing a new addition. I'd studied French for twelve years; French words peppered my thoughts and speech (yes, it's pretentious, but there's nothing quite so specific as *esprit* or *bouleversé* in English). French for me was like an outbuilding, connected to the main house of English by a well-trod walkway. With my Latin studies I had begun excavating a new foundation; I was doing with language what I had done a few years earlier with my physical home.

I'd saved the house's 1840 structure and built on to it. It was not the smartest or thriftiest way to create a permanent, full-time domicile and friends advised simply tearing down the old house, which was of no architectural significance, and starting anew. It would be cheaper in the long run and I could have more and bigger closets, abundant light, and larger rooms. I could build my "dream house." But that is not what I did. When someone would ask, "Why on earth are you restoring the old house rather than tearing it down?" I would become annoyed and repeat my mantra: "Because I'm not a teardown, McMansion girl. I respect the past and do not want to obliterate it." So I excavated a new basement, updated the old house, and added a new wing, all using the architectural vernacular of the old. Language, like architecture, is an ever-evolving structure that we create and re-create throughout our lives. The new always incorporates what came before. No attempts at a made-up "universal" language (remember Esperanto?) have ever taken hold. Nor has classical proportion been replaced by "modern proportion."

Whenever I told a friend or acquaintance that I was learning Latin, those who had taken a bit of high school Latin would happily recite the conjugation of *amo, amare* (to love) like a little poem. My English friend Caroline even had a mnemonic rhyme that her mother had taught her, though it scrambled the order of the inflections and didn't truly rhyme:

Amo, amas
I love a lass
Amatis, amamus
In my pajamas

Amo, amare, amavi, amatus was the first verb introduced in week three. In Latin, four forms of verbs are cited: the first-person singular present tense *amo* (I love), the present infinitive *amare* (to love), the first-person singular perfect *amavi* (I loved), and the perfect passive infinitive *amatus* (to be loved). These allow the student to identify which of the four conjugations governs the verb. As there are five declensions, or noun patterns, so too are there four conjugations, or verb patterns, in Latin.

Curtis said, "Of course you all probably know this verb: probably your parents have recited this conjugation when you signed up for Latin to show you they remember it. However, your parents often learned the wrong pronunciation. *Amo, amas, amat, amamus, amatis, amant* is not pronounced with the stress on the last syllable. Stress in Latin is on the penultimate or the antepenultimate syllable."

So Latin, dead lo these many years, has changed for students over two generations. I once attended a yoga retreat with Kofi Busia, a master Iyengar practitioner who is also a scholar and a wise man. As we held postures, he walked among us, philosophizing, his oft-repeated theme "You cannot change your future, you can only change your past." I'd spent the week, while suffering through extended shoulder stands and downward dogs, trying to get my mind around that until it finally hit me that what he was saying was that how you carry and interpret your past affects everything you do, thus, your future. If a setback made you feel a hopeless failure, you carry that; if you took it as an opportunity to learn and improve, you carry that. Inevitably, in the course of your existence, you will transform the meaning of past experience. And if a new insight arises, a new feeling or a new bit of information, everything might change.

In Latin, the discovery of a poem that uses a word in some way heretofore unused by the known literature can change the dictionary in the future. Everything that moves backwards changes motion forward. I was changing my past even now, by taking Latin. I was excavating a new basement below the linguistic home I'd inhabited since college, pushing the void ever deeper underground.

CHAPTER 3

Language is the only homeland.

—Czeslaw Milosz

When I totaled up commute, class work, homework, and memorization, my Latin adventure was taking up about twenty hours a week. I loved being a student again. I no longer felt as though I were merely killing time in worthless pursuits and cul-de-sac mental meanderings.

As we progressed through the year, the workbook became my sport and pastime. Following each new grammatical concept introduced in the text, the workbook offered drills, rote memorization, and fill-in-the-blank exercises. I loved the workbook. Of the aural, visual, and kinesthetic modes of learning, I seemed to be in the latter camp; writing more firmly planted things in my mind than simply repeating and staring. And I loved filling in the blanks. At the end of each chapter, there were simple sentences to translate, then more and more complex sentences, which used the cumulative vocabulary and parts of speech we had learned. Since our vocabulary was limited to first- and second-declension nouns, most of the sentences were about war (*bellum, belli*), pretty girls (*puellae pulchrae*), goddesses (*deae*), and queens and their islands (*reginae et insulae*). So we began to learn the priorities of the Romans.

Every day when I returned home from class, I spent an hour or so doing the practice sentences in the workbook, even those we hadn't been assigned. I knew I had to work harder than my classmates to memorize; my memory had been altered and addled by so many more years of substances, illnesses, life. Besides, I liked translating the sentences: Cultivating words was as fun as gardening, and it could be done even on cold, rainy days.

While I memorized declensions, George memorized declivities (from the Latin *declivis,* sloping down) in mountains, seeking the best routes for climbing the Catskill peaks. When it was warm, I'd return from class to find him sitting on the porch with his topographical maps.

"Why do you spend so much time staring at maps," I had asked him during the early days of our relationship.

"I'm not staring at maps," he'd corrected me, "I'm studying them."

He also studied weather and wind, which were his only overlords at work and leisure. He planned his days, both work and play, around the weather. George is an arborist, and, in his early sixties, still climbs trees. I've seen him as high as fifty feet, carefully roped in with safety lines, working a three-foot chain saw. In his work, he specializes in finding an expansive view and cutting trees to reveal it. His eyesight is better than 20/20, and he can identify a bird before most people can distinguish it even as a random spot in the sky.

When he is not in trees, George is often hiking in the mountains, and he's happy to drive an hour, or two, or more, to get to them. He is a member of both the Catskill 3500 Club, made up of those who have climbed every Catskill peak over 3,500 feet, as well as the Adirondack 46ers, which welcomes those who have scaled the forty-six peaks over 4,000 feet in the Adirondacks. George likes to be high up, where there is a panoramic vista.

The day after a snowfall, he'll be off with skis and snowshoes, never mind that the temperature in the mountains is barely above zero, taking advantage of what is, for him, a perfect day: alone on the mountain trails he has memorized from his maps. While I explore the crowded past of language, George communes with the wilderness of nature. He is almost my opposite, a man of few words and of calm temperament; a man more conversant with nature than culture.

Most days, as I waited for class to begin, I enjoyed watching the young people come in, observing their interactions with one another, their workbooks and cell phones. Two, Alissa and David, always arrived together, always in the middle of some conversation. Sometimes a student would come in, sit down, and furiously do the homework in the ten minutes left before class began. I always rearranged the desks for my threesome: me, Camilla, and Stella, always choosing the one wooden desk for myself—the prerogative of age, as I justified it. Stella always sat next to Camilla, the three of us like three big birds perched in the southeast corner, a counterpoint to the Three Graces, as I called the boys, who always sat together in the northeast corner. Camilla had wanted to take Latin since she was in the ninth grade. She was a reader, and her public school didn't offer Latin, but she knew enough to equate the language with love of reading. Stella, quiet, and seemingly rather depressed, had taken three years of high school Latin at her Catholic school in Los Angeles, but they had stopped offering it when she was a senior. She was a comparative religion major, "but I know that knowledge of the classics is an essential part of a liberal education," she told me.

Besides Camilla and Stella, I'd had a conversation with only one other student, Jerry, one of the Three Graces, who was among the best students in class. Jerry was a drama major who thought the memorization required in Latin would strengthen the skill he needed for learning dramatic roles. No one else ever spoke to me, although one day, three months in, Tim of the magenta stripe, who always sat two desks in front of me, turned around and asked, "What made you take Latin at this age?"

"Just trying to say alive," I told him. He never asked me another question.

Curtis warned us that the practice sentences in our workbook in no way reflected the reality of Rome. "The prudent queen (*regina callida*) sends soldiers off to war (*bellum*), and to neighboring provinces (*provincias*). And the goddesses are everywhere in the practice sentences. Do you think the matriarchy will persist when we get to the third declension and learn the word for king (*rex*)?" he asked.

At the beginning of class each day, we translated the workbook sentences assigned the day before. We all began to make jokes about the progress of the queen and the powers of the goddesses in our practice sentences, and progress there was. In Chapter V, the first sentences critical of the queen appeared. "Unless the queen can control herself, she won't be able to rule her people" (*Nisi se regere regina poterit, non populum regere poterit*) one sentence declared, and another, "If she fails, I will take up arms and rule" (*Si fallet, arma capiam et regam*).

"They're preparing us," Curtis said, "for the next chapter, when we learn the word for king. The preeminence of the queen will end abruptly."

When I was in college in the early seventies, before there was such a thing as academic feminist analysis, the male-centric Roman view was never identified as such. The feminist revolution, although nascent, had made few inroads into academia. I was in a feminist consciousness-raising group in 1971, but most of our discussions centered on mothers, men, housework, infidelity, and appearance. My biggest concern was distancing my future from the bondage my mother had endured: She had ceded all her power to my father and seemed little more than the slave of our house, a thankless job. Every night my father, planted before the TV, would call to her, "Fran, bring me thirteen potato chips and a glass of ice water"; or "a raw potato, and thirty peanuts"; or "another martini." And bring them she would, stopping whatever she was doing to fill his order, which, if not placed before him exactly as requested, would result in a complaint.

Feminism came just in time to rescue me. I defined myself as "not Mother," which of course was very painful to her, and I disdained her advice about hairstyles, clothing, even language. "I do wish you'd take Latin," she'd say every year during high school, and again during college. "I loved Latin, it was always my favorite subject in school." I think she hoped it might give us something in common, something that would mitigate the growing distance between us. But I didn't consider Latin. I continued my French studies. French was the language Terry studied, so to me French was the language of culture and sophistication, and those were what I was in pursuit of, things Terry represented.

In the one classics class I took in college, a survey course that began with the Greeks and ended with the Romans, the sad plight of women in Rome was not discussed, even when we learned that Roman women had only a single name derived from the male line (*gens*). Thus all Gaius Claudius' daughters were named Claudia, distinguished from one another only by a numerical adjective: Claudia, Claudia Secunda, Claudia Tertia, et cetera, an outrage to any right-thinking feminist. Against my mother's wishes, I never took my husband's last name, but always kept my own. It staked my claim as an independent entity, as any man's equal.

Just after my wedding ceremony, as my new husband and I were preparing to leave on our honeymoon, my mother once again lamented, "I do *so* wish you would change your last name."

Why did she wish that? I was too angry to ask. "Please stop nagging me about this," I said. "It was hard enough having two first names as a child, with all the grief I took from people who didn't believe I knew my own last name. At this point I've earned my name, and it's my name. My identity. Why do you care so much?"

"Well then, just call me Shit," she retorted. "I've been Frances and I've been Fritzie, and I've been Fran and I've been Nicholds and O'Conner and Crowder and Patty, so just call me Shit!"

I was shocked at her outburst. Why did taking a husband's name matter to her so much?

Over the years, I've come to understand. Like a good Roman woman, Mother took on the identity a father, or husband, conferred on her. Her father had decamped when she was a child, and she was adopted by her stepfather; her first husband was killed in the early days of World War II, so that surname didn't endure long. She did what was right for a woman of her station and generation, subsumed herself to the next male, his name and his needs. And too often those male needs left her feeling like shit.

Now in the twenty-first century, whenever women were

treated like shit in the literature, it was remarked upon. Almost daily, Curtis pointed out the sexist aspects of Roman culture. When we finally got to the third declension, along with the king came *vis* (power, force, violence, physical strength) as well as *timor* (fear). *Timor* was masculine, *vis* feminine. What did that say about the Roman concept of masculine and feminine?

There was also *carmen,* which meant "a song or poem," a neuter noun. Always fond of giving us cognates, Curtis said, "You can remember it's a woman's name, but that doesn't help with the neuter, and isn't there a piece of music named after it?"

I blurted out, "*Carmen,* don't you know it? It's one of the most famous operas!"

He looked abashed. How could such an educated man not know *Carmen*? I thought, until I remembered he was only thirty-one years old, grew up in Colorado, attended Dartmouth and UC Berkeley. Why would he know opera? I certainly hadn't at that age. Such moments caught me up short, and reminded me I had forty years on the rest of the class, and thirty on the professor.

The third declension is by far the hardest. First-declension nouns were almost always feminine, second masculine or neuter, fourth masculine, and fifth feminine. Not so the third declension, which hosts all three in abundance. Also the relation between the nominative and genitive in the third declension doesn't always follow the same pattern as the other declensions, with merely a suffix added. The declension includes a number of nouns whose nominative case ends in *s* but changes to *r* in the genitive: *flos, floris* (flower), *rus, ruris* (countryside), *ius, iuris* (law). I would soon learn that *s* turning into an *r* is known as a rhotacism. When an *s* or *z* is surrounded by two vowels, it is replaced by an *r* for ease of pronunciation. The term is, like Latin, highly ambiguous, even self-contradictory, because in a medical context rhotacism refers to an inability to pronounce *r*'s. Indeed rhotic (*r*) sounds are the last to be mastered by most children and are the bane of most stutterers. Perhaps the latter should fancify their condition by referring to it as rhotacism.

The third declension also comprised a subset of nouns known as i-stems. There were no hard-and-fast rules about which nouns were i-stems, though they had different endings in the ablative singular and genitive plural than the rest of the declension. Thus this declension required even more memorization than the others, and to make matters worse, it seemed there were more nouns in the third declension than in any of the four other, easier, declensions.

Latin mnemonic rhymes, commonly used to teach the language to youngsters, are not taught to college students, though I began very much to regret that. Every person I know who took Latin in high school has one or more to offer.

Benjamin Hall Kennedy, creator of the *Public School Latin Primer* in 1866, the revised version of which remains widely used in England, included many rhymes to help students learn gender—most of them for the third declension. My two favorites, which actually helped me, are:

> Abstract Nouns in *io* call
> *Feminina*, one and all;
> Masculine will only be
> Things that you may touch or see,
> (as curculio, vespertilio,
> Pugio, scipio, and papilio)

41

with the Nouns that number show
Such as ternio, senio.

Many Neuters end in *er,*
siler, acer, verber, ver,
tuber, uber, and cadaver,
piper, iter, and papaver.

As difficult as the third declension were the endless *q* words
we had learned by Chapter VII, halfway through the book.
Like *w* words in English, the *q*'s are ubiquitous in Latin, comprising interrogatives, pronouns, adverbs, and subordinating
conjunctions. My bêtes noires were the *quam* words, which
proliferated like rabbits. Finally, I made my own *quam* mnemonic, which I recited to the rhythm of a nonsense camp cheer
I'd learned in grammar school. My "Quam Song" is best
accompanied by stamping feet. I ended it with an id, for old
time's sake:

> *Umquam numquam quamquam postquam*
> *antequam priusquam quoniam quis*
> *quamvis quamlibet quia quid?*
> *quisquam nequiqua, nescioquid, id!*

Translated to English:

> Ever never although after
> before before because who
> however as you wish because what?
> any pointlessly I know not what it!

The chant didn't really help my confusion much, but as the year progressed, whenever a particularly difficult syntactical term was being discussed, I'd chant the quam cheer, sotto voce, to Camilla. Only once did Camilla begin the chant, and we both started cracking up. Curtis stopped the class:

"Ladies, would you care to share your joke with the rest of us?" he asked pointedly. I could feel the flush move up my body. My face must have been beet red. I hadn't experienced such a chastisement since junior high, in my French class, for which I repeatedly received the grade of A/D, D being a bad citizenship mark given for my constant joking to my best friend, who sat next to me. Was I still falling prey to such insecure antics? An aging cutup still feeling the need to prove she was way fun and getting her best friend in trouble?

By semester's end, we'd memorized the first three declensions of nouns, which comprised thirty-eight possible inflections, and all four conjugations of verbs, in six possible tenses, both active and passive, which comprised two hundred eighty-eight possible inflections. There was so much to memorize, and so much ambiguity everywhere. In the first declension, half the cases have the same ending. In the second declension, the same is true, and on and on. One can only wonder if the Latin of the Roman streets (vulgar Latin, from *vulgus, vulgi,* meaning the public, the masses, the commoners) hewed to the inflections, especially since the meaning of the sentence might become clear only at the end, when the verb, usually the last word of the sentence, revealed the syntax of all that preceded it.

The sentences in the workbook were becoming more

difficult, but they were nothing compared to the "short readings" that ended each chapter. These were actual Latin texts, from Caesar, Cicero, Catullus, et al., and though the text even gave us word definitions below the sentences quoted, I often had to spend half an hour just deciphering one line. Cicero, in particular, liked to go on and on without a subject until the last line of a five-line disquisition, and pile up clause after clause before revealing the verb. Curtis had a new refrain: "Ambiguity is everywhere."

I had learned enough Latin words that I began seeing their traces everywhere: Gladiolus, the sword-shaped flower in my garden, was named after *gladius, gladii* (sword), and furtive (as were my glances at Camilla's homework pages) is derived from *fur, furis,* meaning thief. Words became more loaded now that I knew Latin: Repugnant, from *repugno, repungare* (to resist, fight against), gave the English word new force. Dilettante, I now knew, came from the verb *delecto, delectare* (to delight, charm, interest). Insulate, from *insula, insulae* (island), explained in a delightful way that the high R-value insulation required for the geothermal system I installed when I rebuilt my house made an island of its interior. Even automobiles took on new meaning. *Volvo* (two of which George owns—every country man has more than one vehicle) means "I roll." When we learned the fourth conjugation verb *audio, audire,* Curtis told the story of the German inventor of the Audi, named Horch, which is German for "Hark." The designers were not allowed to name models after themselves, but Horch used his knowledge of Latin to skirt the rules: Audi is the imperative for listen, or "Hark!" Latin could be subversive. And it seems to be particularly favored by carmakers: in addition to Audi and Volvo are Stratus, Nova, Maxima, Fiat, Prius, Ultima, Optima, Taurus, Focus, and other models. Perhaps the marketing departments of the auto industry thought Latin names would lend their automobiles a dignified and, dare I say, classic feel.

As an editor, I often used the symbol known as a caret to add a word to a sentence or a letter to a word. I'd always thought of it as a carrot, since the symbol looked like an upside-down carrot, and something about it seemed Elmer Fuddish; but no indeed. It was from the Latin verb *careo, carere*, meaning to lack, be without, be free from. The word "stet," editorial shorthand for "I crossed this out but now think it should be kept in" and written above or below a marked deletion, I learned, means "It should remain as it is," and comes from the verb *sto, stare*, to stand.

And then there were my legal favorites that came to us intact from the Latin: *alibi* (elsewhere), a contraction of *alius*, meaning other, and *ibi*, meaning there; and *alias*, meaning, simply, other. How succinct Latin!

Even the idea of reading took on new meaning. *Lego, legere*, principally means to gather but also to read. And *interlego, interlegere* means to understand: literally to read or gather between the lines. Sometimes the Latin behind English words would spin around in my mind like a whirlpool (*gurges, gurgitus*, from which gurgle), threatening to make every word so dense with meaning and allusion I'd soon be dumbstruck.

***

Before the semester final, I met with the siren Ella to go over the workbook sentences I'd translated that we hadn't gone over in class. She was bright, competent, and kind, though I had scrambled at least a third of the sentences. I often felt a sort of panic because I was working so hard yet making so many errors. I had to remind myself that I wasn't being graded and no one but me had a stake in my endeavor. What did I have to prove? Only that old habits die hard, and I had never been a mediocre student, which, at best, I now was. I was competing with my younger self, and guess who was winning? Perhaps it was a blessing that it was much too late to share my disappointing progress with my mother.

I was the second in the class to finish the semester exam. I had always been a fast test taker; at least I still had that going for me. Insouciant Inez had been the first to leave the room, after only thirty minutes.

I imagine she got an A on the test, though she didn't win the prize. That went to Roberto, one of the Three Graces. Curtis turned the potentially mournful day he returned the final into a sort of celebration, presenting high-scoring Roberto with a bust of Cicero, who, it turned out, had been assassinated on this very day: December 7, 43 B.C. His decapitated head had been displayed in the Forum.

I got 85 out of 100 on the final, which seemed to me reason for my own celebration. Camilla got 92. Stella refused to reveal her score.

We had a six-week break after the term's end. I invited Curtis to lunch. For a Christmas present, I'd bought him the DVD of a filmed production of *Carmen,* which starred Placido Domingo and Julia Migenes-Johnson (who was the opposite of neuter). It was shot *in situ* in the countryside and cities of Spain, and the sexiest opera I'd ever seen.

Curtis and I met at a chic Italian restaurant in Rhinebeck. I asked him about my fellow students, most of whom were entirely opaque to me. Though he didn't name them, Curtis told me that often students choose Latin because they have some sort of learning or social disability. "It allows them to fulfill the language requirement without having to talk much," he told me. "Asperger's syndrome people do particularly well in Latin because they usually have practically photographic memories," he said. "This is, of course, confidential, but you might have noticed how Tim always remembers every exception to every general rule."

After Christmas, I went to Belize for two weeks, as I'd done for the past five winters. My friend, the writer Patrick McGrath, owned a beautiful house on the beach in Placencia, a small, funky, former pirate town in southern Belize, which we rented at a great bargain. My two beloved friends, Judy and Stephanie, were with me. I did not bring along my texts, only my flash cards, which I looked at only once. Latin and the tropics just weren't *concordia*. We spent our days lolling on the beach, drinking rum, reading, and dancing.

It was the first time I had traveled on vacation without an extra suitcase stuffed with fifteen pounds of books: a next-in-line book, a backup book, a backup to the backup book, et cetera. I did bring my Kindle, however, on which I had downloaded a manuscript I was reading freelance to help defray the cost of the trip. The fledgling writer used the word chiasmus on page 10 of the manuscript. I'd learned the word only a few weeks before, so it seemed a lovely synchronicity—except she had misused the word. She'd conflated it with chasm.

Chiasmus (from the Greek *chi*, which is shaped like an *x*) is a rhetorical term that refers to an *x*-like linguistic structure, where the second half of a sentence or text balances the first but with the parts of speech in opposite order: noun, adjective/adjective, noun; or noun, verb/verb, noun. The structure lends itself well to proverbs and was a favorite of Roman writers:

Multa audi; dic pauca.
Listen to many things; say few.

Cum vinum intrat, exit sapientia.
When wine comes in, wisdom goes out.

I loved such fifty-dollar words as chiasmus, but nothing was more irksome than someone misusing them, which is nothing but pretentious by any reckoning. I'm all for jumping on the chance to use an obscure, newly acquired word. But if you don't have a firm grasp of the meaning and nuance of a fancy word, you have no business employing it. Often people make such mistakes because they use a thesaurus (Latin for horde, treasury, storehouse) and fail to subsequently look up the word in a dictionary to check its subtle shadings. How often have I, over the years, looked up specious and spurious, so as not to confuse the two? Twenty times? Forty? Now I am helped by knowing that specious comes from the Latin *species,* which means appearance. Thus specious is the one that means something fallacious that has the appearance of truth. Spurious, from the Latin *spurius* (illegitimate), is the one that means, in the vernacular, bullshit. How many times have I looked up fungible, a word I long to use but have managed to on only one occasion? It's such a slippery word, slippery like fungus, although there's no relation between the two words. Fungible derives from the Latin verb *fungor, fungi, functus* (to satisfy or employ oneself, to discharge, perform), and has nothing to do with the Latin word for mushroom (*fungus, fungi*), even though they look the same. *Vah!* (Wow!)

With *fungus, fungi* you may notice how often English retains the first-person plural form of Latin nouns: *persona, personae* (first declension); *cactus, cacti* (second declension); *axis, axes* (third declension). But in case you think translating just got easier, the first-person singular and first-person plural nouns in the fourth and fifth declensions (except for the few neuter fourth-declension nouns) are identical.

As I was dilating on the above, my friends rolled their eyes. Stephanie said, "You know, Ann, not everybody cares about these things," and went on to suggest that my raps about Latin were private and perhaps shouldn't be shared. She didn't understand that I was not showing off, though it seemed so to her. I was testing the strength of my lifeline. Old insecurities never die. The void still yawned before me, and words were still my tether and safe harbor. Only now some were in Latin.

CHAPTER 4

That was a way of putting it—not very satisfactory:
A periphrastic study in a worn-out poetical fashion,
Leaving one still with the intolerable wrestle
With words and meanings.

—T. S. Eliot, "East Coker"

Second semester began in late January. Winter had settled in, though few of the students seemed to pay much attention to the weather. Dylan of the soul patch often showed up for class in flip-flops, even though it was well below freezing. Once he showed up in what looked like pajama bottoms and slippers. I had overheard he was from Los Angeles (of course, he was probably a surfer, too). He was sexy and aloof, and were I younger, I would have placed myself next to him and tried to get something going. Alas, however, I was the *anus* (*anus, anus*), a rare feminine fourth-declension noun meaning old woman, not to be confused with *anus, ani,* a neuter second-declension noun meaning anus or ring—a rather alarming homonymic Latinism that I decided not to dwell upon.

One fellow had dropped the class (thus losing credit for the first semester), but if memory serves, he was probably failing anyway. A new young woman, a self-confident brunette, joined us just in time for our introduction to the subjunctive (from the Latin verb *subiungere,* to subordinate or bring under). The subjunctive has its own special mood: one that expresses uncertainty or doubt, or anything nonfactual. This case has come down to English, though it is often neglected. Once, a copyeditor tried to remove the subjunctive from the manuscript of one of my authors, because she thought it sounded stilted. The author, who had used it correctly, changed it back. There followed a long e-mail train between the two. Finally the copyeditor wrote, quoting from the copyediting manual *Words into Type:* "However, many clauses introduced by *if* do not express a condition contrary to fact, but merely a condition or contingency. In such cases, the subjunctive is incorrect and betrays the kind of grammatical insecurity demonstrated by 'between you and I.'"

The author was outraged. Equating the use of the subjunctive with confusing the nominative and objective cases? *Eho!* (Whoa!)

The copyeditor and her manual were both dead wrong. As my favorite language expert, Patricia T. O'Conner, says in *Woe Is I,* "If what's being said is contrary to fact or expresses a wish, the verb is in the subjunctive mood."

I believe whether one favors the use of the subjunctive in English is often the result of one's education. And if, as the copyeditor maintained, the usage sounds pretentious to the American ear, that only demonstrates the extent to which our educational system has failed to instill proper usage in students.

There are also independent uses for the subjunctive, such as optative (If only I were young!), potential (This endeavor might make me feel young again!), and hortatory (Persevere!).

I used the subjunctive to e-mail birthday greetings to my friend Patrick in Latin. His three years of Latin in high school were still available in his memory. Because he knew I was learning Latin, he often threw a Latin phrase into his e-mails to me.

Gaudeamus diem natalis tua! Let us celebrate (hortatory subjunctive) your birthday! I usually mess up when I translate from English to Latin, even worse than the other way around, and indeed I had. I should have written *Gaudeamus diem natalem tuam*, because in Latin adjectives must be the same as the nouns they modify in case, number, and gender. However, I discovered that locution was never used in Latin. An Internet search came up with *Felix natalis tibi* (Happy your birth) or *Felix dies natalis tibi sit* (May your day of birth be happy). *Ad multos annos* (To many years) is still used at St. Peter's Basilica in Rome to say happy birthday to the pope, just like the ending to our contemporary happy birthday song, "and many more." The longest, most effusive expression I found is from Pliny, *Ep* 6.30.1: *Debemus mehercule natales tuos perinde ac nostros celebrare* (We ought, by Hercules, to celebrate your birthday just like mine).

There were other categories of subjunctives with resonant names that I'd never encountered in English or French, concepts that themselves suggested life stories. These were not independent but conditional uses of the subjunctive, and promised even more potential drama:

Past contrary to fact (If I had learned Latin in high
    school, I would have studied Greek now.)
Present contrary to fact (If I were an A student in
    Latin, I would be proud.)
Future less vivid (If I keep studying Latin, I may one
    day comprehend this language.)

Future more vivid, which has certainty rather than
uncertainty and takes the simple future tense (If I
study long enough, I will comprehend this
language.)

I loved the concept of the future being more or less vivid
(from *vivo, vivere*, to live), which has to mean more or less alive
in one's imagination. Who named these concepts? Does Latin
imply determination might make it so, as it so often did for the
Roman vision of conquest?

❧

Bleak winter soon held us firmly in its grip. Was it my imagination, or had the oatmeal on offer at the Retreat gotten thin-
ner, and didn't they use to offer granola as a condiment? Even
Dylan now dressed in boots and down.

Along with bad weather came ever more difficult grammatical concepts. Hard on the heels of the subjunctive, the
ablative absolute arrived like a deep freeze. Two of my Latinist
friends had warned about the ablative absolute: "Just wait till
you get to that," they told me. "It will drive you crazy."

The ablative absolute was introduced, along with participles, in Chapter X, to which we turned just after our two-week
spring [*sic*] break in March. A participle is an adjective made
from a verb, such as hearing (*audiens, audientis*), seeing (*videns,
videntis*), or believing (*credens, credentis*). With the addition of
participles, parsing the sentences in the workbook became infi-
nitely harder. The syntax of a word could no longer be determined only from its ending: with participles, one had to look
in the middle of the words for the *ns* or *nt* that identified a
participle.

The ablative absolute is most commonly a participle and a noun both in the ablative case. The syntax is called absolute because the ablative pair is complete unto itself (*ab-solutus,* having been freed from, loosened away), thus unrelated syntactically to the rest of the sentence. For example, *Bibi vinum te dormiente.* (When you were sleeping, I drank the wine.) The participle is called circumstantial because it defines the circumstances that surround the verb (with, when, because, although). Circumstance derives from the Latin verb *circumsto, circumstare,* literally translated as "to stand around." Many of these concise, handy ablative absolutes have come down to us intact in Latin, as in *his dictis* (with these things having been said), *ceteris paribus* (with all things being equal), and *Caesare duce* (when Caesar was leading). Though the ablative absolute can pop up anywhere in a sentence or verse, the two ablatives that form it are steadies and are usually, but not always, seen side by side. For me, it did not live up to its reputation for being impossibly difficult to grasp.

In fact, I liked the ablative absolute, the way it could wrap up entire epochs in two words, then move on: It felt like a no-fault divorce from the main sentence, rather like mine from my second husband, whom I now refer to as my own Ablative Absolute.

Though he had looked perfect on paper—a well-educated and well-traveled journalist, with a deep knowledge of Latin from his years of ecclesiastic studies—he was not perfect in the flesh. He was ten years older than I, had a slumped posture that conveyed a lack of vitality, and an aura of greyness. He had studied to become a priest from age thirteen till twenty-four, making it all the way to the Gregorian University in Rome before he left the Church, along with much of his cohort, during the Second Vatican Council. I often wondered whether the priests had chosen him for the calling because he had a low vitality, or if they had driven the vitality out of him: Chicken or egg? He was wonderfully articulate; Latinate to be sure as he'd had eleven years of Church Latin in one form or another.

Over dinner one night, as we were discussing what I considered the Church's hatred of sex, I asked him, "So, when you were a young priest in training, did you masturbate a lot and feel guilty?"

"No," he said, "I didn't, I followed the rules."

That was alarming. "Did you ever self-flagellate?" I asked hopefully.

"I don't know, Ann, you may be too wild for me," was his only response.

Certainly I was. But I'd thought that maybe it was time for me to stop being wild. Maybe I could use my excess wild to revitalize him. I had enough libido for both of us and trusted its powers. Besides, my nine-year-old daughter, Sophie, adored his eight-year-old son, and after a five-year parade of boyfriends, Sophie and I were both ready to settle down and try to have a normal family. Two months into our relationship, I was besieged. I very painfully and publicly lost my imprint and was dragged through the national press with my skin off. The capper was a front-page article in the *New York Observer* with the headline "Amid 'Pattygate' and Power Plays Simon & Schuster Dethrones Poseidon." The same day it appeared, my apartment was robbed of radio, stereo, and jewelry, including my mother's diamond earrings, one of the few pieces of her jewelry I'd saved. Amazingly, the thief dropped one of the earrings on the floor as he made his way out the window and onto the fire escape. The police told me the burglary was an inside job; so was my professional scandal. I had been set up, but I couldn't talk to the press; I was the sole support of a nine-year-old, and I knew getting into an argument with my boss in the media might get me blackballed. I was alone and scared. I was reeling. The Ablative Absolute pressed his matrimonial suit. I needed something solid to hold on to. I married him.

Although he'd left the priesthood before being ordained, he was a certified exorcist: "I can say *abracadabra* over you and wipe out your devils," he once joked. But it wasn't true: He could not take the devils out of me. I was soon miserable, he was soon angry, and, after one year, I began strategizing exit routes. I was stopped by serial catastrophes—an *aetas horribilis* rather than a mere *annus horribilis.*

I had taken a new, demanding position as editorial director at a different publishing house, which I soon hated. It turned out to be the wrong company for me, and I didn't like being a manager. I just wanted to be left alone with my books, not deal with the problems of eight other editors.

Simultaneously, my father, who had moved to Florida three years after my mother's death, went in for kidney surgery and came out hooked up to a breathing machine, tied to a bed, stuck in some netherworld of unconsciousness, unable to speak for six months. I commuted to Florida every other weekend. He, the "miracle man," got off the machine only to resume his cigarette habit. He died seven months later.

A year after his death, almost to the day, I was diagnosed with a very scary, invasive cancer and lived on planet chemo for a year. When I emerged from my chemical haze, my daughter entered adolescence like a rocket ship exploding on takeoff and had to be sent away to boarding school.

I needed the ablative absolute to enclose those terrible ten years, which I was relieved to think of as an aberration in the complex sentence that was my life. This new grammatical fix allowed me to box them up in an elegant phrase: *Decem annis peractis, iterum coepi vivere* (With those ten years finished, I began to live again). I left my husband, Sophie went off to college, and I moved to a new, part-time job where I had to be in the office only two days a week. So I reversed my lifestyle: I spent four or five days in the country and only two or three in the city. I became a serious Zen student and meditated almost every day. I was practicing slowing down. It was difficult.

Because it's Latin, which always throws a wrench into translation, there are also ablative absolutes without a participle: a noun and adjective, or two nouns in the ablative will suffice—as in *ceteris paribus* (with all things being equal). The perennially popular *mutatis mutandis* (changing only those things that need to be changed) is also an ablative absolute. It applies to law, but also, pointedly, to editing: Once, I found an editor who worked at my imprint changing sentences that were perfectly good, trying to make the novel hers rather than the author's. This, to me, was trespassing. If only she'd studied Latin, perhaps she would have kept her true role more in mind.

Though grammatically complex, the phrase shows both the compact genius of the language, as well as the challenges posed to a beginning Latinist. Both *mutatis* and *mutandis* come from the Latin verb *muto, mutare,* meaning "to change."

Mutatis is the perfect passive participle (ablative plural neuter), literally meaning "having been changed."

Mutandis is the gerundive (ablative plural neuter), which conveys the idea of necessity, hence: "things needing to be changed."

In *mutatis mutandis* the participle has been turned into a noun and the gerundive its adjective. It's taken me only half an hour to figure this out.

Finally April arrived, but rather than the beginning of spring, it marked the endless ending of winter. It was a time when I especially missed the city, where spring usually arrived two weeks earlier and was not encrusted with filthy, never-melting snow. And the streets were busy.

I began going to the city every Thursday after class for a day or two. George didn't mind—he loved to climb the winter Catskills, or ski, or snowshoe. For him, winter was rest time, outdoor time. I found country winter intolerable, although life in the city seemed to be continuing on quite well without me. And the room I rented from a friend for those few days felt nothing like home; the mattress on the pullout bed wreaked havoc on my back, and the cable TV hookup was so byzantine that I soon ceased even trying to turn it on. Had I, in cashing out of the teeming city and moving to the quiet country, made the same sort of mistake I'd made marrying the Ablative Absolute? I had always known that once one "sells out" of New York City, one could almost never afford to buy back in. Was my real life, still in the city, now contained in an ablative absolute *relicta urbe* (after the city was abandoned)? The question haunted me.

Latin had a specific word for winter (*hiems, hiemis*) and autumn (*autumnus, autumni*); spring was *ver, veris* (the same root as *viridis*, green); and summer was *aestas, aestatis*, which is a variation of *aestus, aestus*, meaning heat. Perhaps, no matter what language, we know spring only when green shoots begin springing from the ground and red and yellow buds begin to swell on trees and shrubs. However, none of the above was happening in my garden.

To make matters worse, in class, right after the ablative absolute we were introduced to the active and passive periphrastics, which made the ablative absolute look like a piece of cake. My Ablative Absolute's oft-repeated phrase, *de gustibus non disputandum est* (you can't argue about taste), I now learned is actually a passive periphrastic.

Periphrastic is Greek for "speak around." The active periphrastic is simply the future active participle, which carries an intended action: *Ver saliturus* (spring is about to spring forth).

But the passive periphrastic, which is the future passive participle with the verb *sum*, brings with it necessity: *Nix sole calido liquanda est* (the snow must be melted by the warm sun).

I didn't understand how these constructions got their names: What did they speak around? Even my trusty *American Heritage Dictionary* offered little help, defining periphrastic as "*Grammar* constructed by using an auxiliary word rather than an inflected form; for example, *of father* is the periphrastic possessive case of *father* but *father's* is the inflected possessive case [the genitive inflection, still retained in English], and *did say* is the periphrastic past tense of *say* but *said* is the inflected past tense."

Hah! Who knew English grammar could surpass Latin grammar in complicated forms! Even after banging my head against this conundrum, and fruitlessly searching the Internet, I still don't understand what the English and Latin concepts have in common, or why the Latin concept means what it does. Perhaps the Romans, so attuned to power, simply decided both intent (future periphrastic) and compulsion (passive periphrastic) deserved their very own syntax. Perhaps they thought this mode of expression made their power more polite.

On the morning of April 21, the birthday of Rome, Curtis staged a spring celebration, even though there was nothing springlike about the grey, sleet-spitting day. I think he was rewarding us for having gotten through the participles, gerunds and gerundives, and periphrastics.

He brought in two large boxes of doughnuts, which were passed around the class. We all took one (I chose the toasted coconut, always my favorite). I was surprised that no one took seconds. There were quite a few left in the box. I found that more surprising than the fact that Rome even had a birthday that was still known after all these years. I later learned that April 21 was chosen because it was the day of the festival sacred to Pales, goddess of shepherds. During the late Republic the scholar Marcus Terentius Varro, after much antiquarian research, decided that the official birth year of Rome would be 753 B.C. No one knows exactly why.

The following week a patch of snowdrops and the short, slender reeds of daffodils began poking above the melting snow. Augie began spending more and more time outside: In these early spring days he favored the cement apron of the barn door, which got all-day sun and retained its warmth better than the lawn. The bluebird pair was setting up housekeeping in their blue birdhouse outside the kitchen window, as they did every year, but this year they had to fight off an invading swallow couple, who, in the end, forced them into the house on the outskirts of the garden.

George now drank his morning coffee outside on the patio. It wasn't warm, but he was like a tree, his sap rising and falling with the sun. He'd dress in layers: hat and fleece, long underwear and warm socks, and sit there for an hour or so, drinking coffee, contemplating whatever it was he contemplated. Unlike me, George liked silence in the morning. I usually greeted the day already in the middle of a conversation with myself about something or other with which I often tried to engage him.

"Ann, I don't want to be inside your busy mind right now," he would say, as he retreated to the birdsong outside. It wasn't warm enough for me to sit outside in the morning. So I would take up my conversation with words. There were always new words to memorize, familiar words to be nuanced, and ever more *qu* words to be revisited again and again. There was always a new grammatical concept to fill my *vorax* mind.

In class, we zoomed through the remaining four chapters in a scant month. Finally, spring had sprung, leaping and bounding into bloom, and in the classroom, faces, voices, and vibe were all brighter. Students now chatted before class, comparing notes on senior papers or plans for junior years abroad. Gone was the alienated preclass silence of each student alone in his or her bubble with cell phone or uncompleted homework. The girls were showing off their legs; Dylan was slouching sexily in shorts and wifebeater tees; flip-flops abounded.

On one of the first truly warm days, we had a fire drill. It was like a party, everyone smiling, students from other classes sitting with us on the benches and suddenly green lawns. We lingered even after the all-clear bell sounded, soaking up the long longed-for sun. Finally Curtis herded us in. For the first time, I felt younger than he. I would have stayed outside on that glorious spring day, lessons be damned.

We sped through impersonal constructions, fear, prevention, and result clauses. We skipped many topics, and no one minded: Did we really need to learn the supine, the middle-voice verb, the little-used locative case, and the historical infinitive? The blossoms of the shadblow tree (so named because the tree blooms at the same time the shad run the Hudson) were blowing in the breezes and, on the parklike grounds of the Vassar campus, ancient specimen trees were in profuse bloom. Daffodils, tulips, and grape hyacinth lined the walkways.

What for months had been grey clumps of sticks were now lively with bloom: yellow forsythia, persimmon-colored quince, and the charming pale earrings of artemisia.

At home the passive periphrastic prevailed: There were gardens that must be cleaned and tended (*hortulus colendus est!*), spring clothes and linens to be unpacked and organized, walks to be taken, a life to be lived (*vivendum est!*). Suddenly country life was delightful. Every day another bright bulb bloomed. Life abounded all around me. Maybe I didn't need so many people after all, maybe flowers could dispel loneliness.

Like any student eager for a break from the daily slog of memorization and homework, I was ready for summer, or at least sort of ready. I would lose all my classmates: Camilla would be gone, as would Stella and Dylan, magenta-striped Tim and the Three Graces. Latin class was our only connection. Despite my repeated appeals, Camilla had no plans to continue with Latin; she was committed to being an artist, and between her work-study job, the golf team, sculpture, painting, and core requirements, she didn't have the time for it. But I was determined to continue on taking Latin the following year, though I wouldn't be studying with Curtis, who would once again be teaching beginning Latin as well as intermediate Greek and a freshman writing seminar.

Curtis, delightfully, left us with the longest word in Latin: *Circumnavigaveramusne?* (Had we circumnavigated?) At twenty-one letters it comes in well behind the twenty-eight letters of the longest untechnical, uncoined English word, antidisestablishmentarianism. The Romans had no globe. Perhaps they preferred sailing all the way around their language, which voyage, after a full year's study, I had barely begun.

CHAPTER 5

[Philip] Roth himself has predicted—with excessive gloom, I hope—that before long the reading of novels will occupy a niche not much more significant than the one currently occupied by the reading of poems in Latin.

—Joseph O'Neill, *The Atlantic*, April 1, 2012

The summer was long and I missed the daily occupation of class and schoolwork, so I was happy when September rolled around again. I was beginning my second year with intermediate Latin, a course devoted to Catullus. We were given a more elegant room on the second floor of Sanders Classroom, a long, high-ceilinged, sun-filled seminar room with oversized windows, a well-worn wooden table bearing many scratches but little graffiti, and an assortment of mismatched chairs. The fifty-minute class met at 10:00 A.M. three mornings a week, so I had time for a leisurely breakfast at the Retreat. There I spotted Alissa, a small, unprepossessing girl with long, tangly, mousey brown hair whom I remembered well from the year before.

She starred in the only drama I had witnessed during last year's student interactions. During the first semester she and David (Dreamy David I called him: he had bedroom eyes) appeared to be a unit. Though there were no PDAs, they arrived and left together every day, and always sat next to each other. Then, at the beginning of the second semester, a new student, Kim, joined the class and within days she had turned their duet into a trio, although not for long. After a few weeks, it was Kim and David who arrived and sat together, with Alissa now exiled two seats behind and a bit to the left of them: She could see their every twitch. They must have felt her watching their backs. By the end of the semester, Alissa was again sitting next to David, and Kim was floating solo around the last row of desks.

This year, there were only five of us in the class, four from last year's intro class: Alissa; Charles, a slender, blond Greek major who was now studying Latin as well; tall, gangly, midwestern Roger, the worst student from last year's class, whose father was sticking to his guns and forcing him to take another year of Latin; and me. We were joined by Naftali, a smart, quiet, good-looking freshman who wore a confident expression that announced him to be the smartest boy in the class and, having already had four years of Latin at a fancy prep school, he was.

As usual I was first in the classroom, and as the others arrived, Roger was the only one to greet me. The others focused on their cell phones. Alissa sat next to me, I suppose since I was the only other female in the room. Without saying hello or giving any sign of recognition, she began writing furiously in her pink notebook.

Matthew Wright, our professor, was the year's Blegen Scholar, an endowed one-year research fellowship, which required the visiting scholar to teach only one class per semester and give one lecture. Matthew was from Exeter University in England, a specialist in Greek and Roman drama, ancient literary criticism, and fragmentary and lost works. He loved the tantalizing snippets of Roman and Greek works that came down to us only through references made to them by their contemporaries. They are the obscure of the obscure, though there was nothing recondite about his personality. He was a tall, slender man, in his late thirties, who wore fashionable eyeglasses, a snappy pink dress shirt, tie, and tight blue jeans.

He greeted us with the traditional Latin, *Salvete discipuli,* then handed each of us an old-fashioned, bound, green and grey notebook and a retractable pencil. How lovely! I thought they stopped handing out notebooks and pencils in second grade!

"*Scribite omnia quae dico,*" he said. Now we students stole glances at one another, alarmed and mystified. Matthew repeated, slowly, with hand gestures of pencil writing in note-book, "*Scribite omnia quae dico,*" as we worked out that he was telling us to write down everything he said.

He went on to dictate eight questions typical of "getting to know you" in a foreign language: where are you from, what are your hobbies, do you like music, what is your favorite color, et cetera, and ended by giving us a list of colors, none of which we'd learned the prior year. Matthew questioned each of us in turn: *Quod nomen tibi est?* he asked Charles, who answered hesitantly, *Charles mihi nomen est.*

And there it was already: the dative of possession, which translates as, "Charles is the name for (or to) me." Curtis had remarked upon the inordinate fondness of last year's workbook sentences for this way of expressing ownership, which turned out to be lucky for us this first day of class. We all recognized the locution.

After learning each of our names, Matthew asked each of us a question or two in Latin, and we responded falteringly.

My turn came when Matthew asked, *Nonne cordi est musica*

tibi? (Don't you like music?) His question contained several Latin idiosyncrasies: the dative of possession as well as another roundabout Latin locution to express "like"—there is no word for "like" in Latin; there is love, but to signal that you enjoy something you say *cordi est mihi* (it is to my heart—dative of possession again) or *mihi placet* (it is pleasing to me).

I thought some questions deserved a simple yes or no answer, so I asked him how to say yes in Latin. But, alas, there is no word for yes in Latin. One might say *ita,* which means "the same," or *sic* (thus) or *sane* (indeed, of course, to be sure) or *oppido* (exactly, very much) or *certe* (certainly) or even *est* (it is). The best way to answer in the affirmative is simply to repeat the question without the prefixes *nonne, num,* or the suffix *ne,* all of which signal a question.

And it gets even worse. *Nonne,* a double negative, expects a yes answer, while *num,* which seems more indifferent, expects a no. And there is no single word in Latin for no either. One might say *minime* (leastly), *nullus* (none), *haud* (not at all), or *non est* (it is not). *Non* means not in Latin, it does not mean no. And while I'm at it, there is no independent word for hello: *Salve,* which is the greeting for hello, means "be in good health." And *vale,* which is used for good-bye, means "be strong." *Ave,* which translates as hail! or farewell! does double duty, though it is used only as a morning greeting or as a farewell to the dead; *vale* is used as an evening farewell. What is the mind-set of a culture that has no simple yes and no, hello or good-bye? Would I ever be able to understand it?

I had asked Curtis, over our end-of-the-year lunch, at what point in his studies Latin had sunk deeply enough into his brain so he could think in Latin, as, after twelve years of study, I could think, albeit in fragments, in French. He took some time, then chuckled. "I'm not sure it has yet."

66

After about a half hour of questions and answers in Latin (with brief interruptions for the explanations above), Matthew returned to English. "I like to teach Latin more as one would teach a modern language," he told us. We had already learned, from our Latin getting-to-know-you, that he was English, had never before been to the United States, loved music, and planned to join the Vassar College Choir (he was a tenor). His favorite color was purple (*purpurus*). "I want to give you a more organic way of understanding the language," he told us. "After all, there's absolutely no good reason for any of us to be doing this, so I will try hard to make it fun. And I hope you will find Catullus fun," he added as he handed out the course syllabus, which included the warning: "Some of our poems contain lewd language and sexually explicit subjects. If that will be offensive to you, please talk to me." Well, this was news!

As the class bell rang, he assigned us to read Catullus V, one of the most famous of Catullus' poems, which we had (luckily) translated at the end of the previous year. Unfortunately, I had failed to save the long-labored-over translation I had written out, but having once translated the poem helped nevertheless. As we exited the classroom, no one spoke to anyone else. The spirit of camaraderie and fun was so far absent in this group. I couldn't help but wonder if my presence made them more taciturn.

I loved the poem and came to class two days later feeling I had gotten a good grip on it. It was all about living and loving now, before our brief light sets, and kisses, hundreds and thousands of kisses, then more and more. Matthew didn't go over every line of the translation but asked if we had any questions about the words or cases. We did: *nox est perpetua una dormienda,* which led to a long review of the passive periphrastic (*est dormienda*), which, you may remember, expresses necessity. Last year's final bête noire became this year's first. The line's literal translation is "one perpetual night must be slept," or, in the American vernacular, "when you're dead you're dead forever."

At the end of class Matthew gave us another handout: "Latin Rhythm and Meter." This was a topic, doled out over two chapters in last year's text, that Curtis had skipped entirely. Reading through the handout, I understood why.

The Romans considered poetry to be a form of music, and rhythm was paramount. Latin poetry appropriated Greek forms and scansion. Prosody was fungible. Unlike English meter, which is composed of accented and unaccented syllables, all Latin meters are quantitative, and composed of patterns of short and long vowels. A long vowel is either long by nature (e.g., the first-declension ablative *a* is always long, the nominative *a* always short, and all diphthongs are long) or by position (because it is followed by two or more consonants). There were, of course, exceptions to the long vowel rule—the most confusing of which: a mute (*b, p, d, t, g, c*) consonant followed by a liquid (*l, m, n, r*) consonant does not count as two consonants. And worse still was this note that followed the mute/liquid exception: "There are other exceptions to the rule which are too complicated to go into here!"

In hendecasyllabic meter, used by Catullus in most of the poems we studied (in Greek, *hendeca* means "eleven"), the meter is expressed like this:

$$ūū \mid —u\ u \mid —u \mid —u \mid —u$$

with *u* representing a short vowel and — a long vowel.

Last year's text and workbook had macrons (long marks

over the vowel) marking all long vowels in each word. Unfortunately, these helpful marks wouldn't be seen again in any of our texts. They are learning tools only for beginners, and we were now considered intermediate Latinists.

This year, Matthew told us, we would read everything out loud. He wanted us to hear the poetry, as well as see it. And the one thing about Latin that is completely straightforward and unambiguous is its pronunciation. Each vowel has only two possible pronunciations (long or short), each diphthong and consonant only one. (*G*'s and *c*'s are always hard in classical Latin, though in Church Latin they are soft before *e* and *i* as they are in English. We know this because scholars were able to glean the pronunciation from various writings too complex for me to understand, much less explain.) Compare Latin pronunciation to English, which has abundant possibilities: for example, the English "ough" can be pronounced in ten different ways: rough, cough, drought, though, bought, slough, through, hiccough, hough, lough. In fact, Matthew told us, the odds of correctly guessing the pronunciation of a complex English word are around 26/1, whereas in Latin they are 1/1.

Did that make scanning a poem easier? Not by much. Latin poetry also included elisions when a word ending in a vowel or diphthong is followed by a word beginning with a vowel or diphthong, or an *h*, or when a word ending in a vowel and *m* is followed by a word beginning in *h*. We spent the entire hour trying to scan Catullus V. It wasn't so easy to differentiate long and short vowels. The text Matthew had assigned was a diminutive 3x5-inch clothbound 1970 edition by the renowned Catullan scholar Kenneth Quinn. It was my introduction to the nature of Latin textbooks: 87 pages of poems in Latin, 369 pages of commentary in English. And all in 8-point type, too minuscule for my aged eyes. I had already upped my reading glasses from 225 to 250 and didn't think they went any higher without a prescription. Would I have to study with a magnifying glass? Luckily, I discovered that the Internet offered riches: I could download the Catullus poems in Latin, double-space them, increase the font to 14 point, and go to town.

Monday's assignment was to memorize Catullus V for the next class, which was, alas, only three days away. I hadn't memorized a poem in forty years. And now a poem in Latin! It was both exciting and terrifying. "This will plant hendecasyllabic meter forever in your brain," Matthew told us. "And on your deathbed, when you can't read anymore, and you're bored, you'll be able to recite this poem to yourself, and make yourself happy."

I drove home trying to repeat the first line in rhythm to myself: *Vivamus, mea Lesbia, atque amemus.* (Let us live, my Lesbia, and let us love.) Was memorizing Latin poetry a life? Was it conducive to happiness? Was this enterprise insane?

That Sunday I drove with my friends Harlan, Jeanne, and Margaret to hear Margaret's daughter Manon give a piano recital in Great Barrington, a two-hour drive from home. Harlan, a connoisseur of old Mercedes, was the driver; his wife, Jeanne, rode shotgun; and Margaret and I sat in the backseat, which felt more like a comfortable couch than a car seat. I had brought along Catullus V, printed out, double-spaced, and in 14-point type with the scansion marks above each word. While Harlan and Jeanne and Margaret chatted, I memorized. Finally, halfway to Massachusetts, I began to recite the poem.

Harlan stopped me after line seven. "No more Latin," he declared.

"But I can't get the syncopation in the meter," I moaned. "I'll never get it unless I repeat it out loud, and class is tomorrow!"

Margaret, a composer and musician, took the page from me. "Here's what you do," she said, "clap it out, that's the best way to get the syncopation." She was kind enough to clap out the hendecasyllabic meter with me, and we clapped together, the same pattern over and over (though we substituted stress for length on the syllables) until we were silenced. "ENOUGH!" Harlan shouted, "or you'll have to walk in meter the rest of the way!"

I tapped out the meter with my right foot as I drove on cruise control to Poughkeepsie the next morning. It was a difficult syncopation, but finally I had it. I was thrilled to have memorized Catullus V. I knew if I wanted to keep it in memory, I needed to constantly repeat it aloud, and over the next few weeks, like a proud child with an esoteric piece of knowledge, I would recite it to anyone who would listen. Alas, few would. I seldom made it past the fourth line before I was told, "ENOUGH!" This was, as my friend Stephanie had earlier warned, a private passion, even though Catullus V was a classic love poem in every sense of the word.

On Monday, I arrived at class ready to stand up and recite. Much to my disappointment, Matthew never asked us to do so. Instead he presented all the Catullan nouns for kisses (in order of increasing passion: *basiationes, basium, osculum, suavium*— the first a "little kissification," a locution invented by Catullus himself). By the time we had studied four other Lesbia poems, and witnessed Catullus both passionately enamored and abjectly brokenhearted, we had thoroughly studied the verb "to kiss": *basio, basiare, basiavi, basiatum,* in all its tenses and moods. *Lesbia basianda est!* (Lesbia must be kissed!) is a passive periphrastic. Who could imagine kissing could be used to review verb forms?

Before we proceeded with more Catullus, Matthew spent a week on Catullus' precursors, the most interesting of which, for me, was Laevius—even his cognomen remains unknown. It is believed he composed an *erotopaegnia*—a collection of playful erotic poems. He was also fond of making neologisms: His signal accomplishment, to my mind, was the sesquipedalian, twenty-six-letter *subductisupercilicarptores,* which translates as "disapproves with lifted brows" and beats out *circumnavigaveramusne* by five letters!

The following week we translated Catullus I, the dedication poem, and the famous *passer* poems, Catullus II and III, all about Lesbia's pet *passer* (sparrow). There has been much scholarly disagreement about the true meaning of these poems. In the Renaissance, a scholar named Poliziano put forward the theory that this little bird that frolics on Catullus' beloved Lesbia's lap and calms her deep passion (*gravis ardor*) is a sly metaphor for the male member—sparrows being more than uncommon house pets, and the word "sparrow" in Greek being slang for penis. His theory is buttressed by the last two lines: *tecum ludere sicut ipsa possem / et tristis animi levare curas!* (if only I could play with you as she does, and calm the sad cares of my mind), and by a poem, written by Martial a century and a half later, about his slave boy Stella, "My Stella's pet Dove . . . has surpassed Catullus' sparrow. My Stella is greater than your Catullus by as much as a dove is greater than a sparrow." And in another poem, "Give me kisses, Catullan kisses. If they shall be as many as he said, I will give you Catullus' Sparrow."

In Poliziano's reading, Catullus II is a complaint that masturbation cannot satisfy Catullus the way Lesbia does, and Catullus III, a lament that his member has failed him, and Lesbia is in a weeping tizzy about it.

The theory went out of favor for centuries, until it was revived in the libertine 1970s and began raging anew, producing dozens of scholarly articles. In our class discussion of the sparrow poems, I was the only one to come down decisively in favor of the penis interpretation. "It's sure a lot more fun. And that it's not a pure one-to-one correspondence makes it sly and witty fun," I said. In a moment, I felt my young classmates' eyes turn to me. Perhaps it had dawned on them at last that rather than a *senex severa* (a stern elder, such as was featured in Catullus V), I was an emissary from the sexual revolution of the sixties and seventies. It seemed, indeed, that we elders, Matthew and I, might be the only lively persons in the class!

That evening I was inspired. George and I had been in one of those arid troughs filled with criticism and alienation. I began telling him about Catullus II and the sparrow, whom Lesbia pokes provocatively, and holds to her breast, and knows so intimately. I read the poem aloud in Latin, then translated it for him. Though he loved it when I read him poetry, he'd endured plenty of my set-piece narratives about Latin, and I could tell this rendition was not winning the forgiveness for last night's outburst I was seeking. Finally I told him, "The interesting thing is, lots of people think the sparrow is a metaphor for the penis." There followed one of our most lively discussions ever about a poem. Catullus and his *passer, quale-cumque* (such as it is)—a word from Catullus I—led us into a night of *delectatio amoris,* and luckily I never got the chance to tell him about the lament of Catullus III.

As we proceeded through the poems, I saw more and more similarities between Catullus' Rome and the literary New York of which I was a denizen for so many years. Both strove to embody the same qualities listed in another handout Matthew distributed titled "Catullan Buzzwords": *venustus* (charming, pleasing, of Venus), *bellus* (pretty, handsome, gallant), *lepidus* (agreeable, fine, elegant), *facetus* (witty, elegant, fine), *iucun-dus* (delightful, pleasing, jocund), *suavis* (suave, elegant). As far as I can tell, the above all mean pretty much the same thing. Upping the ante are *salsus* (salty, flavorful), *dicax* (articulate, witty, sarcastic), and *urbanus* (sophisticated, urbane). *Urbanus,* of course, comes from *urbs,* the city, host of most things Catullan. Catullus' urban poems are filled with friends, parties, poetic rivalries, learned conversation, gossip, and romantic (especially sexual) adventure.

His poems are those of a young man; wisdom (*sapientia, prudentia*) was not included among Catullan buzzwords. He died young, probably just before he turned thirty, in 54 B.C. One hundred sixteen of his poems survive him.

Though I continued to deface my old Quinn text with penciled-in translations, I now mostly translated from another volume my friend Lilla had given me. She and her husband, Hank, and George and I had spent a week on Nantucket the previous spring, and she was so impressed with the hours I'd spent translating workbook sentences that she felt I deserved her long-cherished hardbound volume of the poems of

Catullus, copyright 1931. It featured the Latin text of the poem (in 12-point type!) on the recto, with Horace Gregory's English translation on the verso. Each poem was laid out easy on the eyes. It had no notes at the back but was illustrated with elegant pen-and-ink drawings by Zhenya Gay.

I have known Lilla for over thirty years. I worked for her husband, Maurice Girodias, a truly Catullun charmer, on and off for the first eighteen months I lived in New York, in 1975–76. Though we never published a book during my tenure, and moved from office to office around the not-then-chic Flatiron district, always one step away from eviction for nonpayment of rent, it was the most fun job of my life. Girodias was the founder of the Olympia Press in Paris, known to be both literary and licentious: He was the first to publish *Lolita,* Henry Miller, J. P. Donleavy, Samuel Beckett, and other luminaries. He also published pornography—most notably the Traveller's Companion series printed in English for American GIs at the end of World War II. They were small, elegant hardcovers, discreet, appealing packages for pure smut, known among the cognoscenti as DBs (Dirty Books).

The series featured such titles as *Forever Ecstasy* by Tor Kung, *A Bedside Odyssey* by Homer & Associates, and *The Whip Angels* by XXX. Most of the authors were pseudonyms (my favorite: Akbar del Piombo) for serious writers who needed a quick buck. Problem was, Maurice was a lousy businessman, always broke, and paying authors' royalties was not high on his list of priorities. He lost Olympia Press to J. P. Donleavy, who successfully sued for unpaid royalties on *The Ginger Man.*

I found it surprising that Lilla's Catullus volume included the notoriously lewd XVI, though translated with the decorum of the era. Many editions to this day omit the first two lines entirely. The poem begins *Pedicabo ego vos et irrumabo / Aureli pathice et cinaede Furi,* which literally translated means "I will sodomize you and face-fuck you, bottom Aurelius and catamite Furius." In Lilla's edition, Gregory translates the lines, "I'll work your own perversions upon you and your persons." Many scholars leave this, and a few other downright lewd poems, out of their volumes. I suspect my mother never studied Catullus. I can't imagine the Church allowing such poetry to pervert their youth. Even as recently as 2009, during an interview with the well-known contemporary classicist Mary Beard, NPR bleeped out the lines, both in Latin and in English translation.

After Maurice had been banned from publishing in France for ninety-nine years, he moved to New York City and started Freeway Press on some millionaire's investment. Freeway's only claim to fame was Valerie Solanas' *SCUM Manifesto* (published not long before she shot Andy Warhol) and cut-and-paste jobs about Muhammad Ali and Henry Kissinger by Bockris-Wylie, the latter of whom, Andrew Wylie, would later become the brilliant literary agent known as "the Jackal."

Because Maurice had published an exposé of Scientology (only now, forty years later, something that mainstream publishers are willing to do), he was hounded by the sect, which set him up for a marijuana bust. A resulting immigration case was taken up by the courts.

The million he'd been given didn't last long, and, broke and tied up in litigation, he had to scramble to stay afloat. Working for Maurice allowed us, his three part-time employees, as well as him, to keep our illusions—Maurice pretended he had a publishing company, we pretended we had jobs that might lead somewhere. He paid us, sporadically, with the proceeds from selling Olympia Press first editions and Lilla's family silver.

Maurice opened to me the New York world I'd longed for: sophisticated, witty, filled with eccentric characters and louche charm. He and Lilla threw large parties at their SoHo loft, her tony friends from the likes of the *Financial Times*, his leftovers from Warhol's Factory, and never enough food. In Catullus XIII, Catullus invites his friend to dinner, so long as the friend brings the dinner. Catullus will provide all the other entertainments: *meros amores seu quid suavius elegantiusve est* (unadulterated love or whatever is more suave and elegant).

That poem expresses well what working for Maurice was: He provided charm, wit, dazzling stories, and access to the downtown demimonde, if not much financial remuneration. It was at Freeway that I met Humphrey, Ed, and Secret Storm, who would become, in order, my most beloved best friend, my first New York boyfriend, and my first husband. All had attended Yale together and were four years older than I. Humphrey and Ed, like me, worked for Maurice when they weren't trying to earn some reliable money elsewhere, and Secret played music with Humphrey.

Humphrey was a character unlike any I had ever encountered. A witty, theatrical gay man, he had scraggly, chin-length hair and was always dressed in grey chinos, T-shirt, a well-worn tuxedo jacket, and a red silk scarf. (He resembled a scruffy Mark Morris.) A child prodigy avant-garde composer, he was a true eccentric: brilliant and iconoclastic and fond of punctuating his sentences with cartoonish squeals of French, Spanish, German, and Hindi (his early childhood had been spent in India—his parents had both worked for the CIA, though they were long divorced). He knew music from inside out. One evening he sat before me as a Mozart piano concerto played on the stereo and matched his facial expressions to the emotional timbre of every chord change.

He made a star, a superstar, of everyone in his life. In true

Warholian fashion, he mythologized his friends and had a nickname for each: Lucky, Lotus Blossom, Auntie Line, Mouser, Burb, and Rhonda. I was Annie Ekaterina, or when he was especially happy with me, Beauty and Intelligence [*sic*]. The only nickname he used for himself was one given to him by his mother, Doris—Chico. I didn't realize until it was too late that Humphrey put out so much sympathetic energy and encouragement for others that he saved little for himself. He should have been composing, but he wasn't. He was in the grip of composer's block, and he fueled that demon with alcohol.

Ed had been a scholar of classics and philosophy at Yale, a classmate of Humphrey's. He came from an impoverished Bronx Sicilian family and was dark of mien and affect. His father had kept a gun, with which he killed the rats that infested their apartment. Ed was tall, thin, and somber, bearded, half bald. And he was desperately in love with me. I treated him terribly. He was too dark for me, still a sunny, optimistic California girl. As Humphrey's friend Lucky once said of me, "I've never met anyone so lacking in a sense of irony."

I was in love with Humphrey, but he was gay, and I had to find a new way to love him respectfully, which I did. In those days, it was still socially unacceptable to be homosexual, but Humphrey let his gay flag fly. He raised my consciousness and set the template for my perennial need for a gay man in my life.

Romantically, I turned my attention to Secret, who had been named Secret Storm by Humphrey, and whom I found extremely appealing and elusive. We never called him by his real name, which was Robert; he was always uncomfortable with his given name, and over the years he variously called himself Robert, Roberto, and by his last name. But for the first eight years I knew him, until our daughter, Sophie, was born, he was always Secret.

Humphrey also was in love with Secret (as was his habit with heterosexual men), though Secret was determinedly heterosexual. The two played in what they called a "Balinese conceptual rock 'n' roll band" called Chow Chow World War, though Secret was, at best, an amateur on both the guitar and flute he played.

Secret came from an old plantation-owning western Missouri family, had attended private school there, and had finished Yale in only three years, with honors. The family money was long gone, leaving in its wake eccentricity and a sense of superiority and entitlement. Extremely smart, arrogant, and fey, he was an "avant-garde" filmmaker. With a shoulder-length bush of frizzy blond hair, and big pillow lips, he would fling long bright scarves about his neck, masking his native shyness with pretentious bravado. He was part Lou Reed, part Françoise Hardy. And he usually carried with him a Super 8 camera.

Secret Storm had a job teaching filmmaking at City College of New York, and was as much under the spell of Humphrey's bombastic charm as I, so he, too, hung around the Girodias scene. After a time, Humphrey, Secret, and I formed a triangle, all in love with one another, but only two of us being of mutual sexual persuasion.

During much of the Girodias period, I had another, equally glamorous part-time job, in a very different part of Manhattan: the beau monde of the Upper East Side. Two mornings each week I took the subway uptown to the gracious apartment of the urbane Irishman Patrick O'Higgins. He had been Helena Rubinstein's amanuensis and had written a best seller, *Madame*, about his time with her. Now he was writing a memoir about his charming Irish father, Pa. My job was to type up the many legal-size pages on which he wrote longhand. I would arrive around 10:00 A.M. on Tuesdays and Thursdays, and as I sat down at the typewriter he'd ask, "Would you like a little pillule?"

Of course I would. It was a diet pill, low-dose speed. He'd write in his bedroom while I typed in his living room, then he'd make me lunch, which always included a bottle of wine. We'd discuss what he'd written, but mostly he'd entertain me with stories about his life among the rich and famous: Marilyn Monroe, who had lived just across 58th Street from where Patrick still lived and had sometimes dined at his house; the Duchess of Windsor, for whom he often served as a "walker"; as well as many other luminaries, both literary and theatrical (Truman Capote, Norman Mailer, Diane von Furstenberg, Estée Lauder), who were featured players in his daily life.

"When we do the revisions, we'll go together to Morocco and stay with Betty Hutton," he promised. For a few months, I had the best of both worlds.

It was during that heady time that I was notified of my acceptance to graduate school in Berkeley in linguistics, but I was having so much fun, delving into an entirely different sort of study—of New York class and society—that I turned my back on academia for the next forty years.

❧

Two months into class, I needed so many books to translate Catullus that I had to devote an entire table in my library to Latin study. The old, much-weathered oak table from my grandparents' kitchen in Indiana became my Latin table; I imagine my grandfather would have approved that it be put to such use. The table holds a large pencil box with many retract-able pencils and several erasers, my Latin grammar from last year, a more compact Latin grammar assigned for class this year, my Latin-English dictionary, my laminated SparkNotes, and both the Quinn text and Lilla's volume of Catullus poems.

I couldn't rely on the English translations in Lilla's volume, though they helped me get a sense of the poems' subjects. Mr. Gregory had taken great liberties with Catullus, and not only in XVI. For example, in Catullus V, he had changed *malus* (bad man), which referred back to the *senum severiorum* (rather severe old men) of line 2, to "poor fools and cuckolds." God knows where that came from! Perhaps he was revealing his own love trials.

Soon we turned to the pejorative poems in class, of which there were many. Catullus often criticized his fellow poets, other men (and women) about town, and he named names. Some read like the columns in the *New York Observer*, the gossip rag of the media business. They discussed what happened at parties, who was walking about with whom, who stole napkins from a dinner party. The randiness of the poems, if not my classmates, increased as we read more. Along with the words for sodomize and face-fuck, we soon learned the word for fuck (*futuo, futuere*), which led to the words for the homosexual "bottom" (*cinaedus, cinaedi* and *pathicus, pathici*) and, so as not to leave out the ladies, two for whore (*moecha, moechae* and *scortum, scorti*). Here I must note that the latter, though a neuter noun, refers mostly to females. It is difficult to know what that says about Roman sex.

In the Roman world, no distinction was made between homo- and heterosexual men; rather, it was all about perceived power: who penetrated and who was penetrated. A bottom was also considered *mollis* (a little soft) and associated with being female. The Romans seemed to assume that every woman was a bottom.

All this information was received with bland-faced decorum by the still taciturn class. I began to wonder if Matthew was deliberately choosing a run of obscene poems to wake up my classmates and get their juices flowing. Unfortunately, there was no handout for Catullan Obscenities.

We used these urbane, pejorative, and downright dirty poems to review gerunds and gerundives; the rules of direct and indirect statements; direct commands; and my old favorite, the ablative absolute. Matthew gave us an assignment to write a joke in Latin. None of our five were good enough to merit repeating, but two old standbys do: The punning *semper ubi sub ubi* (always where under where) and the reversal of Caesar's *Veni, vidi, vici* (I came, I saw, I conquered) to *Vidi, vici, veni* (I saw, I conquered, I came).

After the midterm (which, being an auditor, I decided I didn't need to take), the class came a bit more to life. Perhaps everyone had scored well, or perhaps we were happy, after a two-week break, to be back with Catullus again. God knows I was! I'd spent the two weeks at home, bored, working on a freelance project and counting the days till class began again. I studied my word list for the semester so far—314 words. I took the typed-up list with me for reading when waiting; since my type-A self was often early for appointments or at least on the dot of time, I spent a good deal of my life waiting. A few favorites stood out: *nugae* (trifles) I could remember as a little candy, *pipio, pipiare* (to tweet) is onomatopoeic, and *fortasse* (perhaps) I just liked. It made possibility sound smooth and sweet, and its long syllables drew out anticipation.

One word, *vegetus,* was a lesson in itself. In Latin it means "lively, vigorous, animated, sprightly"; not, as one would guess from English, its opposite. In Andrew Marvell's seventeenth-century poem *To His Coy Mistress* (a poem clearly inspired by Catullus V), he refers to his "vegetable love." We can be sure he meant lively rather than dull. The *American Heritage Dictionary* states that it was not until the eighteenth century that vegetable, both noun and adjective, came to refer to the plants we associate it with today. None of my dictionaries reveal when the figurative usage synonymous with dull, passive, and still, as in a vegetative state, came to be its primary meaning.

Another favorite of mine is *pervigilo, pervigilare* (to stay up all night), from *per* (through) and *vigilo, vigilare* (to remain alert). That one word held another key to the language for me. Hundreds of Latin words have the prefix *per* to signal "very" or "thoroughly"; *per* is pervasive. *Pervigilo* assumed if you were being thoroughly vigilant, you would be staying up all night: the military culture reflected in the language.

Naftali began speaking up more whenever someone was stumped by a case. Alissa and I now chatted from time to time before class. She told me she had written a fantasy novel. I wanted to be friendly and offer to have a look at it, but I stopped myself. I really didn't know much about fantasy writing, a genre, she told me, she loved as much as she loved Latin. I knew better than to offer to read any novel by a nonprofessional, since so much of my freelance work consisted of the same. And that allows me to throw in another favorite Latin phrase, coined by Juvenal, which working freelance had made me more and more familiar with: *insanabile scribendi cacoethes* (the incurable itch to write, independent of having anything to say).

Charles, the only senior and classics major, was more fluent in Greek than Latin, and now and again offered Greek antecedents to a Catullan line. Roger, the sweet but hopeless economics student, gave his all to his father's injunction (from *in* plus *iungere,* to join or yoke; one of the many definitions of the Latin *in* is "immovable"), but he was hopeless at learning Latin. Though a good memorizer, he just couldn't comprehend cases and syntax, so mostly he struggled.

I often asked the questions the other students were afraid to ask: Is there a word for "give a blow job," or only for "get a blow job"? And indeed there was: *fello, fellare,* from whence today's fellatio derives.

I will leave my poetic semester with the short, enigmatic Catullus poem CV:

> *Mentula conatur Pipleium scandere montem:*
> *Musae furcillis praecipitem eiciunt.*

The penis attempts to ascend the mountain of
    poetry:
The Muses cast him out headfirst with their little
    pitchforks.

CHAPTER 6

Facilius enim per partes in cognitionem totius adducimur.

We are more easily led part by part to an understanding
of the whole.

—Seneca

After a six-week winter break, and my final girl trip to
Belize (Patrick had sold the house), the spring semester
found the five of us Catullans together again. This
semester, I wouldn't have Catullus to substitute for the delights
of New York City. As if to rub it in, our class met in a small, drab
room next to the department offices on the second floor of the
Sanders Classroom. It was long and narrow and crammed with
furniture: The single tall window was partially obscured by a
stained, grey sectional couch, pushed against the wall. The room
had a stale smell, probably from the old Latin texts that filled the
bookshelves lining one wall, or from generations of professors
who had used the couch for napping, and other, perhaps more
Catullan, purposes, leaving their combined scents to ripen.

Roger was already there when I walked into class the first
day. We'd become friendly last semester, since we two were
always the first to arrive. Roger had been worried, at the end
of last semester, that his difficulty with Latin would ruin his

plan to spend his junior year abroad in Denmark. One needed a B+ average to participate in the program, and, truth be told, we all knew he was a D Latin student at best. I had suggested that Roger talk to Matthew about his father's requirement. "After all, he's a visiting professor. What does he care what grade you get, and he's a nice chap; I bet he'll help you out."

Roger had gone home to Kansas for the winter break. I wanted to ask him, but didn't, how last semester's grade turned out. Instead I said, "So, you're still here. Your dad hasn't relented on your Latin?"

"Nope," Roger said. "He's still adamant." I hoped whatever grade Matthew had bestowed on him hadn't ruined his chances for a junior year abroad. Now he had only to worry that this semester's grade wouldn't queer the deal. As the others dribbled in, wriggling themselves between wall and chairs, they positioned themselves in the same configuration as last semester: Alissa and I at the back, Roger and Naftali on the right, Charles holding down the west side. Silence reigned as we awaited the professor.

The sound of determined footsteps preceded him. Bert Lott couldn't have been more different than Curtis and Matthew. While both of them were willowy, scholarly ectomorphs, Bert was a big, blunt-edged endomorph—more Roman centurion than poet, and funny, sarcastic, and iconoclastic. He sat down with a big exhalation and a gusty, "Hello! Welcome! I hope we'll all have a good time this semester." He read off his list of names, as he identified each of us in place.

A very pretty, lively blonde interrupted him with her entrance. "Hi, everybody," she said with a dazzling smile, "I'm Iris, so sorry I'm late." All eyes turned to this breath of fresh air, as she took her place next to Charles, where she remained for the rest of the term. She provided, throughout the year, a bit of sunshine in our drab room. She was always cheerful, always greeted everyone. Unfortunately, her good cheer and friendliness did not prove contagious.

The most fun person in the class was Bert himself, who worked hard to enliven this dull group. "I won't be asking you to write out translations," he said, "but to try to further engage with the Latin, by reading it again and again. I want you to get very familiar with the syntax. We won't have vocabulary tests. Don't know about you, but I never have succeeded in memorizing the vocabulary."

This was news! Bert was in his forties and had obviously been studying Latin for well over twenty years, and *he* didn't have control of the vocabulary! (Although it soon became clear that he did; I think he was just trying to make us comfortable.)

I did not make a vocabulary list that semester. After all, I wasn't taking the finals. I felt I should get the senior's discount of not having to cram for finals, a decision I later came to regret: Had I crammed the second-year vocabulary into my brain the way I had the first year, repeating and repeating and repeating the lists to myself, memorizing, I would have a much better grasp of the language today. A big part of learning any language is rote repetition. Of course this is more difficult with Latin because it isn't a spoken language. It's hard to drop Latin phrases into everyday conversation the way I'd been doing with French for so many years. Besides, I didn't know very many everyday Latin phrases.

Our text was to be *Historia Apollonii Regis Tyri* (*The Story of Apollonius, King of Tyre*). "This novella is a post-empire Roman romance, probably sixth century C.E. We think, like most of the Latin romances, that it's based on a Greek original, but the original has never been identified, nor has the author," Bert told us. "The story, however, has survived tenaciously. It was very popular in medieval times and is thought to be the first romance translated into Old English. Shakespeare freely borrowed from it for both his *Pericles* and *Comedy of Errors.*

"It's not taught too often because most serious Latinist types deem such a romance unworthy of study," he continued. "However, I don't. We don't always have to be so serious! Besides, the grammar and syntax in the novella are quite simple, and it will be easier for you to understand without having to endlessly consult a grammar. One of my goals for this class is for you to be able to reduce the number of books around you when you read Latin, or at least get rid of one of them."

He did achieve that goal, but not for the reason he'd hoped. Instead Naftali shared his discovery of a Web site: the Latin Word Study Tool. Part of the Perseus Project sponsored by Tufts University, it was a pioneering site in the humanities that was news to me. And how happy I was to be introduced to it! It allowed you to type in a Latin word, and the English translation would pop up, complete with possible cases. There was, however, a rub: Perseus was not always reliable and did not distinguish between deponent and nondeponent verbs, so it would label a word passive even when it wasn't. To get the full benefit of the Perseus Web site, you needed to proceed beyond the pop-up definitions and click on the full Lewis & Short *Latin Dictionary* entries. But I didn't figure that out till the following year.

Deponent verbs are yet another of those dismaying aspects of Latin that seem to exist only to trouble students of the language. Deponent verbs are called such (*de* plus *pono,* put down) because they appear to have "put aside" their active forms. Though they exist in all four conjugations, they all have passive forms but active meanings. Such verbs include *fateor* (confess), *conor* (attempt), *sequor* (follow), *morior* (die), and *experior* (experience). If you can find the commonality that makes them deponent, you're a better word analyst than I. To make things even more infuriating, there are also semideponent verbs, which are deponent only in the perfect system of tenses. So *audeo* (dare) always looks passive in the perfect tense (*ausus sum*) but active in the present. And to tie that knot even tighter, notice how similar it is to *audio* (hear).

Apollonius of Tyre was indeed many times easier than Catullus and utterly devoid of literary value. It was, essentially, *The Perils of Pauline* in Roman drag. It wasn't even given the dignity of a bound scholarly paperback. Our textbook was a spiral-bound pamphlet in the "Bryn Mawr Latin Commentaries" series and included twenty-five pages of story and fifty-one pages of commentary. Obviously untouched by any designer, our text was barely worthy of being called a book. As many words as possible were crammed onto each page with narrow margins; the paragraphs were numbered with Roman numerals, each sentence with an Arabic numeral.

The story featured, in order: incest, childbirth, a kingdom won and lost, death at sea, mistaken identities, sudden chance rescues, shipwrecks, love at first sight, lust, greed, skullduggery, abduction by pirates, unwilling whoredom, a kingdom regained, and three different family members believed dead suddenly showing up alive. Happy ending!

It might have been a template for the sort of paperback original I edited when I worked at Dell Publishing in the mid-1970s, both in its lack of artful design and its focus on fast-moving plot.

After Maurice had finally gone totally bankrupt and was contemplating a move back to Paris, and Patrick O'Higgins, diagnosed with lung cancer, moved to Arizona, it was time for me to get a real job. I landed at Dell Publishing. My boss, Bill, had earned his editor-in-chief title by making up a new genre: "The Making of." It consisted of paperback originals that chronicled the behind-the-scenes productions of popular movies. His debut publication was *The Making of Jaws*, and it was phenomenally successful. "Movie tie-ins," novels back-written from film scripts, had already established themselves on mass-market best-seller lists, and Bill had figured out how to take that worthless genre even further. There followed *The Making of The Man from Atlantis, The Making of The Other Side of Midnight*, and *The Making of The Bad News Bears*, in every case, both movie and book equally forgettable.

It was a quick education in popular culture. I hadn't owned a television since I'd moved out of my parents' house seven years earlier. Secret Storm was well educated and tended to avoid anything that might be popluar and American. He looked at life as if through the lens of a Godard film. Lacking any strong culture of my own, I adopted his. We frequented European and Asian films, documentaries, modern art, and performances. We eschewed TV.

Nevertheless, Bill soon figured out that I was quick and willing and gave me one of his paperback originals to edit: *My First 500*, by Babe Bethany, a Los Angeles dame who couldn't write a proper sentence. The three-hundred-page book chronicled her experiences as a swinger (it was 1976, Plato's Retreat was in full advance). The men were numbered and the women lettered—the men reached 500, the women 36 (double J). Many of her sentences ended thus: "we had a very satisfactory orgasm together."

Though I was often plagued by a crisis of meaning and values at work, I knew I was progressing and was finally rewarded with a promotion to assistant editor (though not a raise). I managed to liberate a broom closet and made it my office. The legendary Seymour Lawrence with his eponymous imprint used to stand before my office, which stood alone, windowless, in a long hallway and stare at me, as if my office were a TV set and I were a Charlie's Angel. When I insisted that if he wanted to stare, he also had to talk to me, we became friends, and he became the model for my new ambition: to have my own imprint someday. He also took me out to lunch with Kurt Vonnegut for my birthday, which almost made up for cash twice being stolen from my isolated office, a major catastrophe since I was bringing home only seventy dollars a week.

Soon I was editing most of Bill's paperback original novels. Editing those novels made me an expert on the syntax and tropes of character, plot, and pacing in commercial fiction, much as a story like *Apollonius of Tyre* was perfect for practicing the syntax and tropes of Latin, not to mention the tastes of the mass market of Rome. Perhaps because *Apollonius of Tyre* so lacked style, it was perfect for a refresher course in grammar. The Roman romancers, like those of the seventies, wanted to keep the plot moving rather than stopping a reader with an elegant turn of phrase. At I:4, for example, the ablative absolute and the defining genitive appeared: *cogente iniqua cupiditate,* because an evil passion compelled him (ablative absolute); *flamma concupiscentiae,* a flame of lust (defining genitive); *incidit in amorem filiae suae,* he fell into love for his own daughter. Harold Robbins couldn't have said it better.

We learned that nothing was better at keeping a plot moving with a quick transition than the ablative absolute, which compressed a transition sentence or paragraph into two or three words. The unknown author of *Apollonius of Tyre* threw in an ablative absolute as if slapping the dust of the past off his hands and proceeding on to the next storm at sea, mistaken identity, or abduction, without wasting a sentence.

If only Babe Bethany had known the form: *gaudiis cognitis,* she might have written, rather than "we had a very satisfactory orgasm together," "and then on to the next screw."

As we had learned the different intensities of kisses the semester before, we now learned the different levels of crime, all of which were generously dramatized in *Apollonius of Tyre:* in order of decreasing seriousness: *nefas* (a crime against nature or the gods), *facinus* (robbery, murder, the sort of crime tried in court), *fraus* (cheating or fraud), and *scelus* (an evil deed).

Now, after three or four times reading through a paragraph, and the commentary on it, I could sight-translate when my turn came around in class. The six of us were all at about the same level, except for Roger, poor dear Roger. Inevitably, he stumbled through his translations and mixed up the cases. Often Bert would ask, "What case is this?" and Roger would have to guess each case in turn before he finally hit upon the right one by the process of elimination. Once, as we were waiting for him to stumble onto the dative plural, I had to stifle upwelling laughter—the sort that third graders emit when the dumb kid makes a blooper. Had study turned me back into a child? Was the *senex* the most sophomoric in a classroom comprising three sophomores, a freshman, and one senior?

And what was that laughter about? Was it cruelty, or was it relief that it was someone other than I looking dumb? I was appalled at myself. How could I laugh at poor Roger, my best friend in the class? Who knows what made him so bad at Latin: perhaps it was Freudian, a rebellion again the father's forcing him to take two years of Latin, forcing and failing to make his son love what he loved. Perhaps his father was a transplant from the East Coast Establishment, hoping to keep his culture alive on the prairie.

After spring break, we raced through the end of *Historia Apollonii Regis Tyri*, reading the remaining seven pages aloud in only three classes, with questions and commentary on the grammar. That gave Bert time to talk more about some specific words and concepts. In Latin, many abstract nouns such as *amor* (love), *dolor* (grief), and *sapientia* (wisdom) were derived from verbs. In English it's become common, and annoying, to do it the other way around: viz., those hideous neologisms "to impact" and "to journal" and "to author," and the equally annoying academic jargon "to problematize," not to mention the Latinist phrase "to disambiguate."

Which leads me to a fifty-dollar English word, animadversion, which comes from *animadverto* (I turn my mind to)—from *animus* (mind, reason, consciousness) and *adverto* (to turn to). Apollonius used *animadverto* as a transition between the hero's concerns. He would finish one episode then "turn his mind" to the next catastrophe that awaited him. Why the word came to take on a negative connotation, in Latin as well as in English, even Bert, who knows a lot, couldn't say. The chastising definition is the third listed in Lewis & Short, but the only one that survives into English (NB: Most English dictionaries arrange definitions in order of importance; Latin dictionaries arrange them beginning with the most literal definition and ending with the most figurative). And why did the surviving animus, a neutral, if not positive, noun, take on the aspect of enmity in English? Would I be able to answer these perplexing questions, if, as I had planned before New York utterly seduced me, I'd become a linguist?

That semester I learned that I would have to expand my focus from suffixes to include prefixes if I were ever to master the vocabulary. All the prefixes used in Latin exist in English. Even my House of Ids included one: "perfervid," with "per" meaning thoroughly and "fervid" meaning burning, i.e., impassioned. All the prefixes below also exist as independent words in Latin, as adverbs, prepositions, or both:

a, ab—from, away from
ad—to, toward, against
ante—before
circum—around
cum—together, completely
de—down from, utterly
e, ex—out, away
in—in, on, against
inter—between
ob—toward, against
per—through
post—after
prae—in front
praeter—past, beyond
pro—forward, in front of
sub—under, somewhat
super—over, above
trans—across

A few exist only as prefixes:

dis—apart
in—not
juxta—next to
re—back, again
se—apart

I rebuilt and expanded the house from my textbook to include those words that did double duty, in what you see is a very crowded house. *In* does triple duty as a prefix, a preposition, and a negating prefix, both in Latin and in English. *In* had caused me problems.

They began with another of Patrick's e-mails. He was moving apartments in New York and sent the following: "*Radicitus tollere est insomnium magnum,* or should it be *radicitus tollere insomnium magnum est,* please advise."

Such a question would inevitably send me off on a quest to nail down the translation. Only after exhausting all my own ideas would I allow myself to google it. I loved such challenges and the opportunity for a bit of pedantry. I wrote back:

"As far as I can tell, the word order in Latin can be any damn way you wish, though I prefer the second example for clarity. Insomnia/insomniae is feminine, so I think it would be: *radicitus tollere insomnia magna est,* because insomnia is a predicate nominative.

"Since Latin always prefers gerunds and gerundives to

infinitives, I think it would prefer you to say 'uprooting myself brings me great insomnia,' which would use the gerundive: *me tollendus redicitus magna insomnia mihi affert*.

"Or perhaps better, *me radicitus tollens, magna insomnia est mihi* (the causal participle, with the dative of possessive), probably the best Latin, and my chance to show off!"

Patrick wrote back that he would study my response. "But just on vocabulary, when I looked up nightmare in my *Cassell's New Latin Dictionary*, I got *insomnia*. Can this be right? Having a nightmare is almost the opposite of having insomnia. The French is *cauchemar*, but I don't have the derivation. But it sounds like a Latin-based word (not Greek, anyway)."

I responded that my *Chambers Murray Latin-English Dictionary* gives the following: *somnus, i*, m., for sleep, *somnium, i*, n., for dream, and *insomnia, ae*, f., for sleeplessness. (Why is sleep masculine, insomnia feminine, and dream neuter?) It also gives *insomnia, i*, n., as a bad dream. (And why is that neuter??) *Ecce insomnium!* (What a nightmare!)

I learned another lesson: Never think you understand any Latin word until you've looked it up, and even then, know that it can trick you. *Eheu!* (Alas!) Not to mention, when I double-checked my syntax, I discovered that my suggestion that he use a gerundive was a cat's cradle of errors. Patrick was right in the first place: *radicitus tollere insomnium magnum est* (pulling up from the roots is a big nightmare), and I had wasted an hour being a show-off Latinist.

I was awarded, a few days later, with a perfect word to describe myself: "ultracrepidarian," which means "one who states opinions above one's area of expertise." It was the daily word from the wonderful Web site Wordsmith.org. The word translates literally from the Latin as "beyond the shoemaker."

Pliny the Elder told the story of an ancient Greek painter named Apelles. While viewing one of his paintings, a cobbler pointed out that the sole of the shoe had not been properly depicted. When the cobbler continued to offer comments about other aspects of the painting, Apelles angrily gave the order that the shoemaker should not judge above the sandal: *Ne supra crepidam sutor iudicaret.* Somehow that command was shortened to come down to us in English as ultracrepidarian.

I retreated to the comfort of English and constructed two columns from the many prefixes affixed to the word "pose": not enough for a house, but enough to make elegant pillars.

appose	compose
expose	dispose
impose	interpose
juxtapose	oppose
propose	repose
superimpose	transpose

Apollonius of Tyre also gave Bert the opportunity to explain the Roman system of keeping time when we came upon this expression: *hora noctis silentissima tertia* (the most silent third hour of the night).

The Roman day was divided into twelve daylight hours of unequal duration, depending on the season. A summer hour might last seventy-five minutes, a winter hour only forty-five. The night hours were not divided into hours but into four watches (*vigilia noctis*):

1. *media noctis inclinatio* (in the midst of the bending of the night), also known as *solis occasus* (setting sun)
2. *conticinium* (beginning of the evening)
3. *gallicinium* (cockcrow)
4. *diluculum* (dawn)

Like the Romans, George lived and worked by the sun. As spring arrived, more eager than last year to bestow its glories on our corner of the world, and with it the coming of daylight savings time, George's rhythms of sleep and work began to change. He awakened earlier, dawdled about the house longer, and left for work later. Where in winter his workday began around 1:00 P.M. and ended at dark, by the end of summer it sometimes didn't begin until 5:00 P.M. and stopped at 9:00 P.M. George's days were dictated by the sun, with winter days short, summer days long. While I wondered how timekeeping affected language, George demonstrated the usefulness of the old Roman way.

After our meat-and-potato semester-long meal of *Apollonius of Tyre,* Bert treated us to a brief dessert of Ovid, who would become my favorite Roman poet. But he will have to wait for his own, later, chapter.

CHAPTER 7

Difficile est tenere quae acceperis nisi exerceas.

It is difficult to retain what you have learned unless you practice it.

—Pliny the Younger

Class ended the first of May and, with no outside structure, no reason to leave the house, an excessively long nonfiction book to cut by two-thirds, and another to rewrite, I was at my computer for hours most days, with breaks for walks and weed pulling. I didn't even have to leave my desk to indulge in my new addiction: online Scrabble. You might think my Latin studies would have made me great, or at least good at Scrabble, but no: I lost almost every game. I'd begun playing with accomplished Scrabblists, and soon I was ranked thirty-second among my Facebook "friends"—twenty notches lower than those who had never even played. It was humiliating. One of my friends even refused to play with me again, because the one time she lost a game to me, I sent her rating down ten notches.

I soon learned, playing with my artist neighbor who paints and draws with mathematical intricacy, that Scrabble is as much a visual as a word game—that those who can grok the board and have refined pattern recognition skills are the best players. It's not long, fancy words (or anything less than seven letters) that win the game, but seizing all opportunities to score double and triple points. It's all about where you are on the board, not what you've got in your array. Knowledge of obscure two- and three-letter words is essential, as well as knowing the many uses of prefixes and suffixes to make compound words. Latin should have helped me there, but it took time. I was on a steep learning curve.

I began to cheat. How could I not, with the Scrabble Word Finder a mere click away, instantaneously delivering all sorts of words out of the jumble of letters before me? Many new -id words appeared: ootid, nitid, irid. Most of them, alas, proved unworthy of joining my House of Ids, as they were neologisms created by science, and not in the general lexicon. Nor did I use them in Scrabble. I warned my opponents that I sometimes used Word Finder but had set myself an exclusionary rule: I wouldn't use in Scrabble any word I did not already know, and might come up with myself, had I the patience. Soon I changed that rule to a stricter one: I could use the Word Finder only if I suspected I had a seven-letter word because I had one or two blanks in my letter array. It just wasn't worth the time fiddling with the letters to find it—it was too much like moving around paragraphs in the manuscript I was rewriting, and didn't feel as rewarding as parsing Latin words and sentences.

I set myself the goal of reviewing one Catullus poem every week, though I can't say I was successful. Translating Latin poetry required much the same discipline as editing books. Because Latin allows the writer to place nouns, adjectives, adverbs, and verbs any damn place he likes for the purposes of scansion or emphasis, the words must be moved hither and yon to form a coherent English phrase, much as words, paragraphs, and characters often need to be moved around to make a better book. An editor is, in essence, a scholar of the manuscript she is working on, especially in fiction, in which subtleties must be ferreted out and enhanced, much as they are in Latin poetry. An editor must read a work two, three, four times to help the writer get it right—not so many times as it took me to translate Latin verse, but the deep engagement with a text is similar.

June, my favorite month, arrived. In June, the garden is in its glory and the deer haven't yet made their first feast of everything that blooms. In June, my friend Steve visits for the month, installing himself in the guest room above the barn. In June, I live with both my "husbands," one straight, one gay, the paradigm set so long ago with Secret, Humphrey, and me. Like me, Steve was an editor/publisher who fell victim to the 2008 downsizing. He is also a former Latin scholar. He attended the Latin School in Chicago and minored in classics at Lawrence University. That meant he had studied as much or more Latin than I had French. He is the most indulgent, even enthusiastic, of my friends about my Latin pursuit. He loves to talk grammar and words with me.

George enjoys Steve as much as I do. He knows my relationship with Steve predated mine with him by many years. Not to mention, when he's here, George is allowed to enjoy the quiet recesses of his brain while Steve and I keep up an almost constant chatter about this, that, nothing, and everything.

Since I was failing to translate my weekly Catullus, I decided one Sunday to collect every Latin phrase I came across in that day's *New York Times* (I disallowed crossword puzzle clues).

Here's what I found: *per se, ad hoc, curriculum vitae, ad*

infinitum, in extremis, quid pro quo, habeas corpus, pari passu, and *nunc dimittis.* The latter was used in an op-ed piece by Oliver Sacks. After stating that speaking "no languages but my mother tongue" was one of his signal regrets, he went on to say, "Some of my patients in their 90s or 100s say nunc dimittis—'I have had a full life, and now I am ready to go.'"

And regret he should: *nunc dimittis* actually means "now you are dismissing," or "now you put down." It is the title of a canticle from a text in Luke 2: *Nunc dimittis servum tuum, Domine, secundum verbum tuum in pace* (Now you dismiss your servant in peace, God, following your word). How could the *Times* copyeditor allow so brilliant a writer as Oliver Sacks to employ such a loose translation just to throw in a fancy Latin phrase? Though one could argue that, if one knows the full verse, the two phrases convey a similar meaning, we ultra-crepidarians are very persnickety.

Which leads me to the word *absquatulate* (to depart in a hurry, to decamp, to die), which a friend had recently sent me as a present. It, however, is a mock-Latin word made from *ab* (away) and *ate* (to act upon) affixed to either end of the made-up Latin stem *squatul* (to squat), so it literally would mean, "to go off and squat elsewhere." This word comes from nineteenth-century midwestern and western American attempts to sound learned. Perhaps, since Oliver Sacks laments knowing no language but English, he should have used *absquatulate* rather than *nunc dimittis.*

That exercise clearly revealed that Latin is not a dead language but an undead language—a ghost shadowing many of our words, a zombie showing up in sentences, haunting the living language.

Perhaps Latin as a zombie language can become the latest

teen craze, zombies and ghosts being all the rage in movies and books. Latin is even au courant with the new categories of gender. Clearly the neologism cisgender comes from the Latin preposition *cis,* meaning "this side." It must have been inspired by the Roman concepts of cisalpine and transalpine (our side of the Alps, and the other side of the Alps). So a cisgender identifies with the genitals she or he is born with, while a transgender identifies with the opposite. What would the Romans have thought of a world without a normative gender?

Latin even haunts comedy. The opening credits of John Oliver's HBO show, *Last Week Tonight,* feature thirty-seven Latin and fake Latin captions, from *tempus fugit* under an hourglass, to the made-up *Hostus Mostus* under an illustration of John Oliver, to *insanus maximus* for the state of Florida.

One day I invited Curtis to lunch with us. Though he was still being put through the tortures of Job, interviewing for tenure-track positions while hoping that one might open up at Vassar, Vassar was finding various ways to keep him on. Curtis remained my touchstone, the young man who had allowed my life new purpose: my Latin father and son. He was also kind enough to suggest he give me a tutorial on all the Latin study aids available on the Internet. And I knew he and Steve would enjoy each other.

Curtis was funny and wry, untroubled by Augie, who fixed himself before him and longingly stared as Curtis ate his hamburger: Augie always figured the guest was the easiest mark. Curtis was unflappable, serenely ignoring Augie while we discussed obscure parts of speech.

Over the special rhubarb cake I'd made for dessert, Curtis

offered a new one: the epexegetical infinitive, in which the infinitive explains the subject ("epexegesis" means additional information or explanatory material). The example he gave us was "Cake is good 'to eat'" ("to eat" being the epexegetical infinitive).

Curtis also recommended Basil Gildersleeve's *Latin Grammar*, the *summum* of Latin grammars in English, which included every recondite usage and was replete with the sort of footnoted explanations he and I loved. Gildersleeve was the top American classicist of the nineteenth century, as well as the inventor of graduate school in America.

Curtis was my only source of gossip about the students and professors at Vassar. I was relieved to learn that the dullness of our cohort the previous year was well known and often lamented among the professors of the department.

I asked if Curtis happened to know the fate of dear Roger and if he was able to get the grade he needed for his junior year abroad.

"Bert made a deal with him," Curtis said. "He would be generous with his grade with the proviso that Roger never take another class in the GRST department as long as he was at Vassar."

We all burst out laughing. What a brilliant solution, at one stroke both sparing professors a classical dullard and obviating any future demands Roger's father might make about classical studies.

After lunch Steve retired to his guesthouse, knowing this was a lunch with a learning agenda. I turned the conversation to my latest passion: adverbs ending in *-im*. Like the adjectival English -ids, most adverbial *-im*s were back-formed from Latin nouns ending in *-us*. They seemed to me the first worthy successors I had found to the -ids, though so far I had only ten of them. Curtis gave me a few new -*im* words, then we moved to my computer, where he showed me a site, the Packard Humanities Institute, that contained all Latin literary texts written before A.D. 200. It offered not only a word search and an author search but also a concordance. The latter allowed me to type *im#* and, *abracadabra,* up came all the places where an ancient author used a word ending with -*im*. This was a momentary thrill, with one ruinous problem: The search turned up 42,818 instances of such words.

I consulted the first few pages: 95 percent of the entries were *enim,* which means, variously, "for, for instance, namely, in fact, I mean." It was a very popular word. Also among the -*im*s were the forms and subforms of the first-person subjunctive verb *sum, esse* (to be), in its many tenses, such as *fuerim* (I should have existed), *possim* (I should be able to), as well as the first-person perfect subjunctive ending of all verbs in the second, third, and fourth conjugations and the numbers eleven through seventeen, from *undecim* to *septemdecim.*

I allowed none of the above onto my list. The -*im*s were clearly quite a bit less exclusive than the more selective English -*id*s. I would later discover, when I read Apuleius' *The Golden Ass,* that he, too, was inordinately fond of -*im*s. He even made a few up, and it took only one usage by a classical author for a word to be included in the Latin lexicon.

Using the concordance for enlarging the -*im*s, I realized, was rather like using the Scrabble Word Finder. I vowed not to consult the concordance again, to add to my list only those -*im*s I come across in my reading or conversations (in Latin, haha-hahha), though sneaking a quick peak at it now and again has proved irresistible. Soon I had enough for an addition to my house: the *Im* Shed.

	acervatim	
affatim		articulatim
baccatim		caesim
certatim		confertim
confestim		ductim
efflictim		festim
granatim		incursim
interim		olim
ossiculatim		passim
paulatim		privatim
sensim		statim
summatim	tuatim	verbatim

Over the next two days, there followed an e-mail exchange between Curtis and me. "Would *Bona placenta est edere* (Cake is good to eat) be a proper translation of your example of the epexegetical infinitive?" (Yes, friends, *placenta* means "cake" in Latin!)

Curtis responded that I would need to make my meaning more clear with word order—"the epexegetical infinitive usually follows immediately after its adjective. So it would be something like *placenta est bona edere*. But I'm afraid that the example I gave you may not be idiomatic Latin. You can now check me on stuff like this: if you look up the adjective *dignus* in Lewis & Short you will find that it can be used 'With inf.': e.g., in Horace *dignus describi* (worthy to be described). And if you look up *peritus* it too is used with an infinitive, as in Tacitus' *peritus obsequi* (skilled in submitting oneself [to another]). And if you look up *aptus* you will find that Ovid describes an *aetas apta regi* (a period fit to be ruled). But if you look up *bonus -a -um* you will not find any uses of it with the infinitive. So I'm afraid you need a different example sentence. My fault."

I decided to try again: "How about: *Mala placenta est edere seni et pingui* (It is a bad thing for an old and fat person to eat cake)."

As always, Curtis had another correction: "This sentence can be rescued by a simple change: *Malum placentam est edere seni et pingui.* Personally, I feel a Roman would say it in the plural, *senibus pinguibusque,* and I think he would find a more stylish place to put the datives. Perhaps: *Placentam edere senibus pinguibusque est malum.*"

I showed the exchange to Steve, which led to a long discussion about the true differences between the editor and the scholar: the editor is a dilettante flitting from one subject to the next dictated by whichever manuscript is up next, whereas the scholar digs deeply into one bit of soil, learning every molecule of its composition and what role each might play in a plant's growth.

QED: Nothing in Latin is as simple as it may appear, and true scholarship is very time-consuming.

In early July, Steve left, and I was back to work on rewriting manuscripts. July and August were always long months for me, with no structure but whatever I had scratched together for myself. Though I loved summer, I might have wished it shorter. Steve had told me something he always remembered, that his tenth-grade Latin teacher, Ruth Nelson, had taught him about July and August.

"When Caesar reworked the calendar beginning in 44 B.C. and Augustus finished the project after Caesar's death, each renamed the month of his birth: Caesar substituted July (*Julius*) for *Quintilis,* and Augustus renamed *Sextilis* August. They wanted to make sure their months were among the longest, so they each stole a day from February. Since it was the most dispiriting month, no one minded."

I researched this assertion. The old calendar, which Julius Caesar replaced, had comprised 12 lunar months and 355 days. That calendar had begun at the spring equinox in March (*Martius,* after the god of war). Even then, February was the odd month, consisting of 28 days, a number considered unfavorable and thus appropriate to the month designated for purification (or for us who live in the Northeast, the most unendurable of the months, which we are grateful is a bit short). The new Julian calendar began in January and consisted of 12 months and 365 days, with February adding a "leap day" every four years. To make up for the days missing from the shorter calendar, two extra days were added to January, August, and December, and one extra day was added to April, June, September, and November. So Ruth Nelson was partially correct: Augustus did get an extra day, but Julius had his from the get-go.

Unlike the elegant economy of the language, the way the Romans counted the days seemed ridiculously cumbersome. Perhaps because their inflected language had so accustomed them to reading backwards, Romans counted days backwards, too. There were three fixed points in the month from which they counted: the Kalends, the Nones, and the Ides. The Kalends was the first day of the month; the Nones (named such because they were nine days before the Ides) were either the fifth or seventh day of the month. The Ides fell on the fifteenth if the month was long, and on the thirteenth if the month was short. The day before the Kalends (or Nones or

Ides) was called *pridie* Kalends or *ii* Kalends, the day before that *iii* Kalends, et cetera. Therefore my birthday, March 22, would translate as *x* Kalends April, or as abbreviated in a Latin text: *a.d. x Kal. Apr.* (a.d. is the abbreviation for *ante diem* which means "before the day").

On a.d. *ii* Ides July, *Gildersleeve's Latin Grammar* arrived: 567 pages in densely packed 8-point type, a forbidding volume that might well have contributed to giving the study of Latin a bad name.

Paging through the beginning, which was much like most grammars, laying out the parts of speech, the declensions, and conjugations, I was thrilled to find on page 123 "Formation of Words." First, there were two pages on the formation of substantives, ranging from agency (indicated by endings of *-tor, -tric, -trix*), diminutives (*-lo, -la,* and *-lus*) and, behold, on page 127, a list of "The Suffixes in Detail," which gave a breakdown of Latin nouns and adjectives arranged by suffix: Out of 250 entries, not one -id appeared. Adding insult to injury, Gildersleeve didn't include adverbs in "The Suffixes in Detail," so I learned no new *-im*s.

I decided to rest my brain with a game of Scrabble. I scored my highest word ever—unstrung—for 131 points. And believe it or not, I found it all by myself.

CHAPTER 8

Disce quasi semper victurus; vive quasi cras moriturus.

Learn as though you will live forever; live as though you
will die tomorrow.

—St. Edmund of Abingdon

My third year of studies was one of consolidation and
consolation, poetry and lost possessions. Fall semester
I studied the lyric poets at Vassar, spring semester
Ovid at Bard. James Romm, the Latinist at Bard who didn't allow
first-year auditors, had contacted me in August through Facebook
of all places, wanting to consult with me about his book, which
had been recently published, and the next on which he was working. At the end of our meeting, I reminded him, "You probably
don't remember, but I contacted you two years ago about taking
your beginning Latin class. I've since been attending Vassar."

He didn't remember that e-mail exchange but said, "You're
clearly a serious student. You're welcome to audit a class with
me at Bard if you like."

Since I'd already asked permission from the professor at
Vassar, Rob Brown, to attend his lyric poetry class, I stuck to
Vassar for the fall but used James's kind agency to shorten my
winter commute and study Ovid at Bard with his colleague

Ben Stevens during spring semester. It would be like my junior semester abroad. How odd that modern social media facilitated expanding my ancient pursuit.

I was now taking 300-level classes, the advanced level. The lyric poetry class at Vassar was larger than last years' intermediate classes: There were seven students, including me. Only one student, Naftali, was there from last year—Alissa had gone off to Rome for her junior year abroad, and Roger, having fulfilled his indentured Latin servitude, wouldn't be seen again in the department. It was explained to me that the advanced classes are often bigger than intermediate because some students come to them in their freshman year, after having taken advanced placement courses in high school.

We had two freshmen: Bethany, the first black student I'd seen in a Latin class, and Siobhan, a quiet young woman who hid behind her hair all semester and never spoke unless she was called on. There were three seniors: a gay young man with the Shakespearean name of Yorick who minored in drama; a gracile redhead who, as it would turn out, was a worse Latinist than I, even though she was a major about to graduate; and a flamboyant blonde, who, even as the months progressed and it got colder and colder, dressed in retro Madonna, with some part of her bra always showing. A small diamond sparkled from her left nostril. Madonna and the other seniors obviously knew one another well and squealed with delight when tall, lanky Ralph, a sophomore, whooshed in just before the professor.

This semester I was no longer the lone *incana* in the class. Rob Brown, an elegant Brit who'd been in the United States long enough to lose all but a trace of his accent, was my age, though he had not yet gone entirely grey. A full professor, he was a typically contained Englishman, who seemed to know everything about Latin poetry. He dressed elegantly, in neatly pressed pastel shirts and pants, often with the secret pizzazz of brightly striped or polka-dotted socks. Rob had met and married an American during a brief stay in Washington in the early seventies, and, after returning to England for a few years to get his PhD, had resided in the United States ever since. He was the senior member of the GRST department and was only two years away from retirement. He was the most formal of the professors and also the most rigorous in making certain his students truly grasped the syntax of each line we translated.

Rob began the class with a disquisition on lyric poetry (so called because it was always accompanied by a lyre) and its provenance from Greece. We would begin with Catullus (again!) and then move on to Propertius and Horace. To warm us up, Rob handed out Catullus LI, which is based on a Sappho poem.

Ille mi par esse deo videtur,
ille, si fas est, superare divos
qui sedens adversus identidem te
spectat et audit
dulce ridentem.

We had studied that poem last year, but as I struggled to remember what *identidem* in line 3 meant, Madonna effortlessly translated:

This man seems to me to be like a god
this man, if I may say it, seems to surpass the gods
who, sitting opposite you beholds you again and again
and listens to you laughing sweetly.

It's a passionate poem, a jealous poem. Catullus goes on to describe his senses ripped from him, his tongue stilled, his ears ringing, and his eyes covered with night. I love the internal rhyme of *identidem* and *ridentem*—the ambiguity of Latin that allows the adverb *identidem* to refer to the man looking again and again, hearing again and again, or Lesbia laughing again and again, thus making Catullus even more jealous. The way Latin has the freedom to place words where they are polyvalent enchants me. As difficult as the system of inflection may be, it allows an author to place a word where it will enhance the meaning, often doubly or triply (as in *identidem* above). It allows an author to make his poetry dance a tarantella.

Rob assigned Catullus I, II, and III for the next class, a mere two days away. The cover of the Catullus text we were using that semester featured a large illustration from Lilla's textbook, Zhenya Gay's line drawing of Lesbia cradling her *passer* in her hands. The ever-present past, again became present and future.

I was back with the inspiring *passer* poems, but rather than feeling inspired, I panicked. Though I remembered the poems well, lots of the vocabulary had lapsed from my memory in one short year. I looked at the Horace odes, to which we'd be turning later in the semester. *Heu!* (Alas!) The first poem was entirely opaque until I'd reread it three times, as well as the eleven pages of notes in the back. There was at least one word per line (more often three) that I didn't know and only a few lines that I could translate entirely without the dictionary. I already knew, and would be reminded throughout the semester, that it would take me many sorties through a poem to come up with a translation I felt at all confident about. *Eheu!* (enhanced Alas!)

Did I really want to spend three hours a day translating? I

was afraid this might happen. Perhaps I should demote myself to the intermediate classes for another year. I put the Horace away, deciding I disliked him, and spent the next day pondering what to do. I figured the prof who was teaching Vassar's intermediate class would let me audit, since I was now a known quantity in the department, but what if she said no? Should I reconsider Bard? But wasn't that to be an advanced class also?

My mind ricocheted back and forth obsessively: Should I challenge myself in advanced Latin or consolidate in intermediate? Should I first leave one class and then try to enter another, or *vice versa*? Alas, thinking of that phrase soon sent me down another rabbit hole. Every time I came into contact with a Latin phrase, I had to analyze it syntactically, adding even more confounding problems to my dilemma.

Vice versa is an ablative absolute: the past tense of the verb *verto, vertere* (to turn about), and the noun *vicis* (which has no nominative form and means "change, interchange, alteration, condition, fate," or in its transferred, metaphorical form, "position," thus doubly enacting the expression). *The American Heritage Dictionary* declares *vicis* comes from *vix,* which it doesn't—*vix* being an adverb meaning "hardly, only just, or scarcely." A search through four different Latin dictionaries turned up no noun *vix, vicis,* so obviously even the estimable lexicographers of *American Heritage* were *vertuntur* (spun around) by this expression. *Webster's Third* defines *vice versa* as "with the alteration being changed," taking into account both the ablative absolute form and the preferred definition of *vicis.* I decided to stick to that one.

Unpacking that expression took me forty-five minutes, demonstrating forcefully why approaching advanced Latin had left me spinning about (*vertebar*) for a day. I could, of course, impose my own limit to homework, two hours a night perhaps, if I wanted. What did it matter if I was the worst in the class? I wasn't being graded. Studying Latin was just something I had devised in order to have something to do, I didn't have to beat myself up about it. What was I trying to prove?

I decided to visit Professor Brown (should I call him Rob without asking?; he was, after all, a contemporary) before Tuesday's class. As I approached his office, I felt like a trepidatious sophomore.

He stood from behind his desk and welcomed me. Undone by his courtly graciousness, I blurted out, "I'm not sure my mastery of Latin is up to the level of your course," as I approached his desk, "and I certainly don't want to be any sort of drag on the class."

"Oh no," he reassured me, "you'll be fine. Not all the students are as advanced as they may appear. Bethany and Siobhan come straight from high school. Don't worry. We'll be going over the translations each day in class, and I always find an older, experienced person has a lot to offer a class of undergraduates."

What could I say? I felt stuck. "Here, sit down and share my doughnuts," he offered, motioning to the chair next to his desk and sliding a Dunkin' Donuts box in front of me. I could see the multicolored tops—pink and green glazed, sprinkled, sugared, and cinnamoned.

"As you can see, I like doughnuts," he confessed. "These were left over from this morning's Beginning Latin class. I find a little sugar at an early hour helps at the beginning of a semester."

As I picked out the toasted-coconut doughnut, and tore it in half to demonstrate my womanly self-control, Rob asked, "Tell me what brings you to Latin study?" So I told him my story, in brief.

He was particularly interested in my publishing past. His daughter had briefly worked for a notorious female publisher who herself had gone to Vassar. His daughter didn't last long; few of that particular publisher's assistants did. Rob had heard many stories of extravagant expense-account use, foul language, sexual shenanigans, bitter competition, and female feuds. Par for the publishing course, I told him.

As we walked to class together, he once again assured me that I would do well, reiterating that he very much wanted me to stay in his class.

Feeling somewhat encouraged, that evening I fortified myself with the admonition Catullus gives himself at the end of poem LI, in three stanzas not inspired by Sappho:

Otium, Catulle, tibi molestum est
otio exsultas, nimiumque gestis
otium et reges prius et beatas
  perdidit urbes.

Leisure, Catullus, is dangerous for you
too much leisure transports you
    and you run off the rails
leisure has laid waste to kings
    and their once wealthy cities.

I knew that leisure would be my downfall, too. The specter of my mother playing endless and lonely solitaire games during the last years of her life, and her drinking, which started earlier and earlier in the day as the years progressed, haunted me. I memorized those cautionary lines: *Otium tibi molestum est,* and soldiered on.

After the next class, Rob assigned a secondary source on Catullus for us to read, accessible online, but only in the library. For the past two years, I'd felt like something of an interloper at Vassar and used the campus only for classes and to get breakfast at the Retreat before class. I entered the Frederick Ferris Thompson Memorial Library for the first time by walking under an expansive London plane tree, one of whose wide branches extends fifty feet over the sidewalk, as if nature herself had provided a beneficent arc to formalize the library's entrance. Admission tours claim that the limb holds the title of "longest unsupported London plane limb in the world" in the *Guinness Book of World Records,* though no one has yet been able to find it there.

The library itself looks like a cathedral: It is an imposing stone building in the Perpendicular Gothic style, with crenellated turrets, leaded-glass windows, and a verdigris copper roof. Up the marble steps one enters a grand hall at the back of which glows the splendid stained-glass Cornaro window. It portrays Elena Lucretia Cornaro-Piscopia, the first woman ever to receive a doctorate (in 1673), defending her dissertation on Aristotle before her professors at the University of Padua. Her dress is grey, with a sash of pink satin. At its founding, Vassar's colors had been grey and pink, though in 1974, when the college began admitting men, they changed to grey and burgundy so as not to force the male students to wear pink (even though a large portion of them were and are gay). The sweatshirts and T-shirts have lost their charm; the new colors look common, unlike the more elegant old ones.

The lights in the tracery of the Cornaro window represent

Grammar, Dialectics, Music, Philosophy, Astronomy, Medicine, Geometry, and Theology, the linchpins of the humanities, before my generation had a go with "relevance."

From that first visit onward, I went to the library for an hour or two before class to finish my homework. The computers there provided access to many online Latin translation tools. Rob Brown had even given us a link to a Horatian Odes vocabulary Web site, from which one could make flash cards or listen to a computer voice saying each word and its definition. I did not use that Web site. It made me feel less like a scholar, and the computer voice was grating in the library's hush.

I decided to think of the library as my new office; in comparison, even my swankest publishing office—a large corner on the fourteenth floor in Rockefeller Center—seemed ordinary. There were never more than six or seven of us at the wooden tables, which could accommodate forty, and two of the regulars were grey-hairs like me. Were they auditors or professors? I never worked up the courage to ask.

We began with Catullus IV, a poem about a boat, *fuisse navium celerrimus* (once the fastest of ships) that *nunc recondita senet quiete* (now ages in its retired repose). It reminded me of myself, my fast career, and its end. If only I could age in retired repose. But I couldn't. That's why I was here.

In several poems, Catullus criticizes his friend's lovers, always in terms of their looks. He was a man of his time, entirely sexist. In poem XLI he writes:

> *Ameana puella defututa*
> *tota milia me decem poposcit*
> *ista turpiculo puella naso.*

That totally fucked out girl Ameana
demanded ten thousand of me
that girl of yours with the ugly nose.

He's even more outraged in XLIII, when others call that
same woman lovely and compare her with Lesbia:

Tecum Lesbia nostra comparatur?
o saeclum insipiens et infacetum!

My Lesbia is compared to you?
oh how tasteless and stupid our age!

His assessment of Varus' girlfriend is more obliging: *non sane
illepidum neque invenustum* (not, indeed, unattractive or without charm). This, we learn is a *litotes* (Greek for understatement)
or damning with faint praise, a favorite device of Catullus. The
neoterics strived to make liberal use of such Greek poetic devices.

Rob refers us to XLIII, where Catullus really goes to town
with litotes:

Salve, nec minimo puella naso
nec bello pede nec nigris ocellis
nec longis digitis nec ore sicco
nec sane nimis elegante lingua.

Hello, girl with the not little nose
with the not beautiful foot, nor black eyes
nor long fingers nor dry mouth
and speech not very elegant.

Catullus also liked *hyperbaton* (Greek for "stepping over"):

Totum ut te faciant, Fabulle, nasum.

So they might make you, Fabullus, all nose.

Here *totum nasum* (all nose) surrounds the rest of the sentence like two nostrils.

Thus we began to acquire yet another language, which comprised poetic terms, most of them Greek: *litotes, hyperbaton, anaphora* (rhetorical repetition for emphasis, as in *Otium . . . Otio . . . Otium* in poem LI above). Many more poetic devises uniquely suitable to Latin would be arriving with Horace, who made copious and artful use of them; and then next semester, Ovid would blast them into rock 'n' roll.

Catullus often uses diminutive versions of nouns: *versiculus* (little verse) rather than *versus; turpiculus* (a bit ugly) rather than *turpis; libellus* (little book) rather than *liber;* and *ocellus* (little eye) rather than *oculus.* I loved that one could simply add *elo* or *ulo* or *ellus* or *culus* to make a word diminutive, much as Patrick O'Higgins had done with his "pillules." He must have known Latin.

English does the same with "ette." I often referred to myself as George's wifette, because I'll never formally marry again: I'm too old to be a girlfriend, lover is too intimate a display, and partner too businesslike. Perhaps I should adopt Catullus' expression *deliciae meae* (my sweetheart), though the fact that it's always plural, and always feminine, is troublesome.

Several diminutive forms have been handed down to English, the most alarming: *mus, muris* (mouse), which becomes *musculus* (little mouse) in its diminutive form, and from there travels to English to become "muscle." The thought of little mice running up and down my arms was almost enough to make me stop exercising!

We also learned the fascinating and very useful concept of "inalienable possession." In Latin, as in other languages, a possessive pronoun is unnecessary before a noun of inalienable possession because those things are so much a part of you that they will always be yours—name, genus (family, class, community), body parts, coughs, shadows, spirit, breath, seedlings, and domestic animals. Husband and wife as well as in-laws are included along with blood kin. The most surprising inclusions are leader, president, and governor. I loved the concept of something so clearly belonging to you that you didn't need to declare it, and did so only to emphasize your possession. It got me thinking about my own inalienable possessions, which were mostly absences: two former husbands, with accompanying in-laws and stepchildren, dead friends, dead parents, estranged siblings, a career and an identity as an editor and publisher, not to mention the signal accomplishment that launched both of the latter, which I had been forced to sign away twenty-five years ago.

In the spring of 1978, I left Dell for a new job as senior editor at Pocket Books, the paperback division of Simon and Schuster, though I was hardly qualified for the position. The publisher at the time, Peter Mayer, was committed to hiring bright young people.

Soon after I arrived at Pocket Books, Humphrey, still my best friend, who had been working for a literary agent for the past two years, gave me a short, 98-page manuscript. It was, as he put it, "awful and fabulous." It was my first purchase at my new job and his first sale as an agent.

Flowers in the Attic, by V. C. Andrews, was the tale of four children locked in an attic while their mother attempted to win her way back into her rich father's will. The children were overseen by their grandmother, who called them the "spawn of the devil." Their mother had married her cousin; the incestuous relationship resulting in her being disowned. The children, Chris, thirteen, Cathy, twelve, and the five-year-old twins, would be sequestered in the attic of the family manse, for only a couple of days, Mother promised, until she had won back her father's love. Days stretched into months, months into years. Finally, Chris and Cathy have sex, one twin dies, and they escape.

Humphrey and I were both captivated by the novel. We also goofed on it: Maybe it would become a camp classic and Humphrey could march in the Halloween Parade dressed as the evil grandmother, with me playing the mother. We never imagined that it would become not only a camp classic but also what can only be called an "awful classic." It launched my career and one of the most successful franchises in publishing history. Though V. C. Andrews has been dead since 1985, a book bearing her byline comes out like clockwork every year, sometimes twice a year: There are now over seventy in all.

As soon as it was published, *Flowers in the Attic* hit the *New York Times* best-seller list. I was sent down to Portsmouth, Virginia, to meet the author.

"Don't eat the doughnuts," my colleagues warned me. (In the novel the children are given the "treat" of doughnuts covered with arsenic-laced powdered sugar, which is what eventually kills one of the twins.)

I did eat the doughnuts. Virginia's mother presented them, on a crystal plate, along with a pitcher of water covered with a clean linen napkin. Virginia was amused, watching me looking warily at the doughnuts. "I told Mother we had to have them," she said. "Mother hasn't read the book."

Mother had been Virginia's caregiver and prison warden from the time Virginia was fifteen, when a fall led to surgery, which led to arthritis, and, finally, paralysis of her spine from neck to coccyx. Virginia reclined, rather than sat, in a type of wheelchair I'd never seen before—rather like an ironing board with large wheels and leg rests. When she wrote, she would alley-oop herself out of her chair using a trapeze that hung from the ceiling, and stand leaning against a chest-high table for support. She typed on a red IBM Selectric and always dressed for work. "I think it makes me more creative," she declared.

For the next six years, Virginia and I cranked out a novel a year, on a crazy-fast schedule, which required me to become more of a co-writer than simply an editor.

Fortunes changed. The novels became the best-selling paperback originals ever. Virginia called me her Fairy Godmother. I called her my Golden Goose. And Humphrey and I shared a somewhat preposterous, somewhat scandalous author. Virginia became a wealthy woman, moved to a large house overlooking the Chesapeake Bay in Virginia Beach, and bought herself a customized wheelchair and a van so she could hire herself a driver to squire her around town.

I parlayed my success into a hardcover imprint at Simon and Schuster, though I'd never published a hardcover book. In the heroic mode of deluded grandeur, I named my imprint Poseidon, the Greek god who drove Odysseus on his ten years of wanderings. I identified with both the driver, on the rampage from old passion, and the clever, driven hero. Like him, I had managed to navigate between the Scylla of power and the Charybdis of sexism to make my own way at Simon and Schuster.

For my logo I chose the sea horse: one of the few aquatic animals whose female lays her eggs in the male's pouch and leaves it to the male to carry them to birth. Was it odd to name my imprint after a male? Since I was a young woman in a world where the males held all the power, it seemed appropriate.

In October, a week before Halloween, lanky Ralph appeared in class dressed as a centurion in full Roman legion regalia: red tunic (*tunica*) bordered in gold and covered by a leather cuirass that ended in lappets (a skirt of decorated leather strips). Over that he wore a *cingulum* (military belt) and *lorica segmentata* (metal armor, segmented like a beetle's back, that covers shoulders and upper arms). He also sported a red *focale* (scarf) and a *paenula* (red hooded cloak). A golden laurel band festooned his hair, and a sword was strapped to his *cingulum*.

We all gathered around him, delighted and impressed. Where did he get such a costume? He told us he'd found the cuirass on eBay and his mother had helped him make the pleated skirt.

When Rob entered the room and saw us all standing around, he enacted my favorite longest word from the previous year: *subductisupercilicarptores*. Then Ralph stepped out from the surrounding circle and displayed himself, at which point Rob broke out into delighted, if subdued, laughter. It was our most fun class ever, a Roman legionary in our midst, but still we translated! It was not yet Halloween, but we were a class of Romans on that day.

The next week we left Catullus for Propertius, who was of the next generation of Roman poets. Though heavily influenced by Catullus, Propertius confined himself to elegiac verse. He is known as one of the most difficult of the poets to translate. His use of Latin is deemed experimental by many classicists; he mixes vernacular with high literary Latin and expresses his feelings in elliptical, sometimes paradoxical lines, often imposing intellectual scrutiny on deep emotion. He is also extremely fond of including obscure mythological references, whose bearing on his own plight is often strange and ambiguous. His poems often seem like jagged mosiacs of feeling, his emotions ricocheting from the depth of misery to the height of ecstasy.

Love, for Propertius, is a siege that he is powerless to repulse. In the very first poem, we get a taste of his misery in love, as well as the difficulties in translating it into English.

Cynthia prima suis miserum me cepit ocellis
contactum nullis ante cupidinibus
tum mihi constantis deiecit lumina fastus
et caput impositis pressit Amor pedibus.

Cynthia was the first to capture me with her eyes
miserable me, untouched before by any desire
until her eyes slayed my habitual arrogance
and love trampled my head with his commanding feet.

Propertius' fondness for participles (*contactum, constantis, impositis*) is the least of what makes him vexing to translate.

After Propertius came Horace, commonly considered the best of the lyric poets, though I did not immediately love him. Perhaps because he was the class-climbing son of a freedman, many of his poems toadied to Augustus. And his tone, which of course we can't truly know, was *superbus* (haughty, proud, arrogant). Unlike our suffering, passionate, occasionally turgid Catullus and Propertius, Horace's voice is stately. He was moved more by philosophical musings than emotions. Formally, he was a virtuoso, writing in almost every meter and genre of the Greeks, and made innovations in all of them. Horace seemed never to doubt himself, never to suffer the tempests of loves. Instead he handed down wisdom as if from on high:

In Ode I.1:

Me doctarum hederae praemia frontium
dis miscent superis, me gelidum nemus
nympharumque leves cum Satyris chori
secernunt populo.

The ivy garland, privilege of learned brows
unites me with the gods above
the icy grove and the nimble chorus of Nymphs with
    Satyrs
distinguish me from the common crowd.

No *nugae* or *libelli* (trifles or little books), as Catullus called his poems, for Horace. Instead gods, demigods, and nymphs dance just for him. Nevertheless, there was no mistaking his great artistry as a poet: In the line above, nymphs and satyrs are placed so the words lightly dance together. The word placement enacts the scene.

Horace was also a master of the poetic figure *zeugma*, from the Greek for "yoking together," which is when one verb has multiple objects, each with a different sense of the verb. Here it is in Ode I.9, which became my favorite of Horace's poems:

Nunc et Campus et Areae
lenesque sub noctem susurri
*conposita **repetantur** hora*
nunc et latentis proditor intumo
gratus puellae risus ab angulo
pignusque dereptum lacertis
aut digito male pertinaci.

Now the fields and courtyards
are **sought again**
at the trysting hour at dusk
and now the low whispers are **repeated**
now the telltale happy giggles of the girl
hiding in the corner are **renewed**
and the token snatched
from her barely resisting arm or finger is **claimed**.

Repetantur does quadruple duty as a verb: meaning first "sought again," then "repeated," then "renewed," then "claimed," as in the translation above. Of course such syntactical acrobatics make translating Horace all the harder. The same poem also uses this line: *donec virenti canities abest / morosa* (while morose greyness is far away from you, blooming).

Rob points out that *virenti* (blooming) is used for youth and *canities* (grey) for age and asks, "Now are those metonymy or synecdoche? I always confuse the two."

Even Rob Brown, after thirty years of teaching Latin, still confused metonymy and synecdoche! His question was an island of relief in a sea of Greek.

Ralph came to his rescue. "They're metonymy." He explained that metonymy is when one thing, which is closely related, is substituted for something else, as in "glass" or "grape" for "wine" (with Horace, as with Ralph, it always came back to wine). "Synecdoche is a part standing in for the whole, or vice versa, as in *ferrum* (iron) for sword." Make that wine and costume.

That one line gave us much to discuss. *Morosa* comes from the noun *mos*. *Osus* or *osa* added to the end of a noun makes it mean "full of," as in our English vernacular expression fabulosa. *Mos, moris* in the singular means "custom" or "practice" or even "law." In the plural, *mores* means "character" or "personality." Thus character is a collection of customs and habits. *Morosus* means full of *mores* and translates as "stubborn, hypercritical, gloomy" (like the English word "morose"). Too much custom, practice, or character can become toxic. *Babae!* (Wow!) What lessons can be learned from a single word of Latin!

Perhaps it was Horace's fondness for the grape that made him somewhat morose. Just before his most famous line in Ode I.11, the oft-quoted *carpe diem, quam minimum credula postero* (seize the day, putting little trust in what will come next), he advises his friend, *sapias, vina liques, et spatio brevi spem longam reseces* (be smart, pour the wine, and, our span being brief, trim back boundless hope).

The man liked to drink. As often as he anticipates death in the poems, he also exhorts his interlocutors to bring out the wine, sometimes going so far as to specify region, vintage, and glass size: *deprome quadrimum Sabina, O Thaliarche merum, diota* (I.9) (Thaliarchus, pour out the four-year-old unmixed wine from the Sabine wine jar).

Whenever a reference to drink was made in Horace's poems, Ralph cheered, lifted an imaginary glass, and mimed drinking. It's probably no surprise that he did not finish the semester.

Now, when I feel fretful of an afternoon, rather than

breaking out the wine, I translate. I must be entirely sober to translate. I'm always happy when a friend who knows I'm now a Latinist sends me an e-mail, asking me to translate a line. A writer friend asks what a line used in that week's *New Yorker* means: *Absens non erit haeres*. *Non erit* means "it will not be." *Absens* means "someone absent or far away." My online dictionary tells me that *haeres* is second-person singular imperative of the verb *haereo, haerere* meaning "to hang, cleave, stick to."

So I try: The absent will not cling? Do not cling to the absent? But *absens* is nominative, so that can't be right. Finally I give in and google it. "An absent person will not be heir" is the translation.

In none of my three Latin-English dictionaries does "heir" appear as *haeres*, though on the Internet it does appear as an alternate spelling of heir *(heres, heredis)*. How on earth did Latin students not break out the wine daily without the Internet?

The next morning at the Retreat I ran into Tom Beller, a writer acquaintance who had attended Vassar and was giving a reading that day. We began discussing Latin, and I told him the above story, which led to his telling me about his grandfather's heavy, carved wooden armoire, which Tom had shipped from New York to New Orleans. "It sits like a fortress in my office," he said, "and takes up way too much room, but I can't bring myself to get rid of it." And here, serendipitously, is the noun's relationship to the verb: inheritance as clinging. Clinging and letting go, inalienable possessions and transitory possessions, those would become the bêtes noires of my next two months.

My past was suddenly rushing back at me. Within a day of each other, two e-mails arrived in my mailbox. *Flowers in the*

Attic was being remade as a Lifetime TV movie with two former movie stars and an up-and-coming young TV star. The first e-mail was from a Young Adult novelist wanting to interview me for a new blog, *The Toast,* curated by women in their forties. Women who came of age in the late seventies/early eighties were the largest contingent of the V. C. Andrews cult, and with the announcement of the film, the Internet was awash in things V. C. *The Toast* was devoting an entire day to her.

The second was from the popular Web site BuzzFeed. The writer was preparing an in-depth article on the posthumous V. C. Andrews phenomenon.

Five years after her death, I had been forced to sign away large sums owed to me on her posthumous books, as well as to the franchise that I thought would be the inalienable posses-sion, not to mention financial engine, of my career. I was legally enjoined from telling which books published after her death were or were not written or conceived by her, and what my role was in their conception and writing. I had allowed myself to be painted as an extortionist and with no little determination had moved on. And here it was coming back again. The past is always present, especially in the Internet age. I became possessed—read: obsessed—with this inheritance wrested from me so long ago. Was it time for me to change the past, claim my inheritance, and clear my name? Did anyone but me even care?

For days I pondered, tormented, raged. Should I write a book, a wrathful chronicle about a young woman being screwed by men who stole what she had created? Finally, on the advice of a savvy publishing lawyer, I decided to let the past lie. There was, however, one inheritance I could recover: I could resurrect Humphrey, who had been written out of the story long before I had.

Had Humphrey lived, the scandal would never have

occurred. He would have told the truth and protected me. Humphrey died in 1982, four years before Virginia. He had turned thirty-three only a week before. Though we didn't realize it at the time, so new was the plague, AIDS killed him, and quickly. What started as two days of hiccups progressed into a month in the hospital, a face and body Day-Glo yellow, a stomach as big as a woman's carrying triplets, dark eyes void of their usual warmth, shockingly distant and weary. It was the look, I later learned, of death.

His mother, his boyfriend, my long-unseen former boyfriend Ed, Secret, and I attended him at the hospital every day for that month, as piece by piece his body shut down. I rehearsed daily the declaration of love I wanted to make him and daily gave him long foot massages instead. It allowed us both to believe we were still who we had been, California Ann imposing some touchy feely on her best friend, Humphrey. It was then, perhaps, that I finally understood and embodied irony.

The call came on a wet, grey September morning, at four thirty, the hour of the wolf, that hour between night and dawn when most people die and nightmares are most real. The sky wept on us as we made our way to the hospital. The nurses knew us; they had left the body bag unzipped, knowing we'd want a last glimpse of him. Humphrey looked, in death, nothing like he had in life.

That visitation was the only memorial we had for him. Though the agent for whom he worked hosted a gathering, I didn't attend; it was the sort of event I would have attended only if Humphrey would go with me.

⟡

Horace, it turned out, perfectly suited my revisiting that first death, so young, and I began to like him much more. I chose for my class presentation at the end of the semester Ode I.28, a poem about death, which, for once, Horace writes about without the consolation of wine. Horace first lists all the renowned men who have died: astronomers who measured the skies, beloveds of the gods, heroes of Troy, all *morti concesserant atrae* (consigned to black death). He even appropriates lines from Catullus V, that poem that uses death only as an impetus for kisses: *omnes una manet nox et calcanda semel via leti* (the same night awaits us all and we all must tread once the road of death).

The last lines of the poem kept me thinking about Humphrey:

Quamquam festinas, non est mora longa;
licebit iniecto ter pulvere curras.

Although you are in a hurry, the delay is not long;
after three covering handfuls of dust, you will be
allowed to run along.

Humphrey's body, after our visit that sad morning, was donated to science, neither buried nor burned. There was no box of ashes, no plaque commemorating him. All these years later, I regret that no memorial was held for him. I was too young, back then, to understand the power of a formal, public farewell. Although he's been dead well over thirty years, this V. C. episode and the opportunity to talk about him with *The Toast* and BuzzFeed reporters brought him back again. If my accomplishment could be taken from me, my beloved, now-dead friend was forever an inalienable possession.

Winter break began the second week of December, and as always, I dreaded it. Winter in the country always feels like exile to me, and that winter the snows arrived in early December, along with an unusual cold snap, a harbinger, I feared, of a brutal season to come. I began counting the days until what would become my annual Florida escape, just after New Year's, for two weeks. To accompany my elegiac funk, I bought a copy of Anne Carson's *Nox*, which is a brilliant translation, meditation, and reenactment of Catullus CI, Catullus' elegy for his brother. Carson describes *Nox* as "an epitaph (for my brother) in the form of a book."

As much artifact as book, its accordion-folded pages rest in an elegant 6x9-inch box. The first page is the text of Catullus CI smudgedly printed on antiqued paper:

Multas per gentes et multa per aequora vectus
    advenio has miseras, frater, ad inferias,
ut te postremo donarem munere mortis
    et mutam nequiquam alloquerer cinerem,
quandoquidem fortuna mihi tete abstulit ipsum,
    heu miser indigne frater adempte mihi.
nunc tamen interea haec, prisco quae more parentum
    tradita sunt tristi munere ad inferias
accipe fraterno multum manantia fletu,
    atque in perpetuum, frater, ave atque vale.

Carried through many lands and many waters,
I come, brother, for these sad rites,
that I might finally give to you the honors of death
and speak in vain to your silent ashes
since fortune has taken you from me.
oh pitiable brother, so unfairly taken from me.
now, however, in the ancient custom of our ancestors
accept these sad gifts

made in tribute to the shades
take them, dripping with a brother's many tears.
and forever, brother, hail and farewell.

As *Nox* continues, each word of the poem is translated on
the verso; as words repeat, their definitions become longer, and
darker, and *nox* (night) encroaches on them. On the recto are
vestigia (traces) of Carson's brother—photos, drawings,
stamps, and bits of letters. It is a collage of memory, meditation, speculation, and mourning.

"Prowling the meanings of a word, prowling the history of
a person, no use expecting a flood of light," Carson writes.
"The luminous, big, shivering, discandied, unrepentant, barking web of them that hangs in your mind when you turn back
to the page you were trying to translate."

Like Catullus' poem, *Nox* is Anne Carson's *munus* (service)
for her brother. The book is metonymy and synecdoche: Every
dead person is a dead language, and every memory a translation.

When I returned home, I pulled out from its bookshelf
Private Parties, a book Humphrey wrote while a senior at Yale,
in 1969, as a birthday gift to his mother to help her understand
his music. It pictures the *vestigia* of Humphrey. *Nox* had
brought it vividly to mind. Like it, *Private Parties* is *sui generis,*
utterly original and formally inventive. The now-tattered,
black-leather-bound, 5x8-inch artist's notebook holds a story
composed in the spatial manner of a musical score, with cal-
ligraphy, pictures, drawings, and musical notation. Lively,
funny, filled with Humphrey's singularly sweet absurdist
humor, it is the story of a journey he takes with his friends,
enlivened by the visual personification of his musical intelligence.

Erudition as play, dazzle, and spark. *Private Parties* is the dead language that was Humphrey.

When *The Toast* and BuzzFeed articles were posted, there was, finally, my *munera* for Humphrey M. Evans III, written back into the story: three handfuls of dust for my dearest dead friend.

CHAPTER 9

For philology is that venerable art which demands of its
votaries one thing above all: to go aside, to take time, to
become still, to become slow; it is a goldsmith's art and
connoisseurship of the word which has nothing but deli-
cate, cautious work to do and achieves nothing if it does
not achieve it slowly.

—Friedrich Nietzsche

In my next class, transformation replaced possession and
loss. The spring semester, which began in late January
when spring was still two or three months away, I would
be taking a class at Bard, studying Ovid, and I knew that Ovid
was all about transformation: He was the poet of love, and what
is love but transformation?

The evening I returned from Florida, George presented me
with my belated Christmas present. I had been disappointed
when he had told me at Christmas, "I have something very,
very special for you, but it's not ready yet. I promise it will be
when you get back from Florida." I had badgered him to tell
me what it was: I always want to know surprises immediately
and have a hard time not leaking hints and more hints if I've
found a present I think the recipient will especially like. As a

teenager, I used to sneak open my Christmas presents under the tree.

It was a cold, sunny day. "You have to come outside with me to get your present," George insisted. "It's hidden."

I was skeptical; last Christmas George had given me thermal socks and a chair that tilted back for sky- and stargazing. The year before I'd been presented with a headlamp for night hiking and a pair of cleats that strapped on to boots for safe navigation over ice. His presents were suggestions of activities we might do together. Mine were likewise trying to work a transformation on him. One year I bought him a $600 New York–style briefcase to replace his tattered brown one. He tried it once, and ever since it's been stowed under the upstairs bed; he still uses the old one, now even more tattered. I have, however, used my stargazing chair, my headlamp, and cleats. I live here now. I've learned to buy my own jewelry.

"Put on layers, it's cold," George said. He wears lots of layers; sometimes, when he's working outdoors in winter, three or four. I've resisted giving in to the country necessity of long underwear and instead simply stay indoors most of the winter. Augie misses his walks, but often the roads we walk are icy, Augie's paws get cold, he soon insists we turn back, and I don't really mind.

Skeptically, I donned undershirt, sweater, wool pants, socks, boots, jacket, hat, scarf, gloves, then George ushered me out the kitchen door and up the rocky rise past the abandoned playhouse in the woods. Sophie used to play there, but it's been a brambly unused part of the property for years: The stone bear that once guarded the playhouse is a crumbling relic, the door off its hinges, the glass long gone from the windows. Beyond the ramshackle structure, a rock seam rises and tapers to a narrow ledge, with a steep drop to a vernal stream far below.

George had cut a path through the brambles to the top of the cliff. He insisted I close my eyes as he took my hand and led me up the rock seam. I was already cold when he finally said, "Okay, you can open your eyes."

There were the two battered old chairs I'd been nagging him to take to the dump, positioned in a freshly cut clearing at the edge of the rock cliff. Just as I was about to say something less than kind, he rested his arm on my shoulder, and said, "Now, turn around."

ECCE! Before me was a salmon-colored sunset sky with a thin blue cloud stretched like a Caribbean island above the distant, purple Catskills. Suddenly, we had a vista of sky and mountains! I was amazed.

"Sit down," George beckoned to the chairs, "enjoy the view."

"How did you do this?" I asked. Our property is surrounded by forest; its rock ridges and hollows, lovely as they are, limit any view of the sky, even in winter. I've always felt overly landlocked here, missing the expansive view of the Hudson and western sky I enjoyed from my New York City apartment. Now mountains and that same western sky were revealed in the middle of our forest!

"You know how I always walk around up here and you can't figure out what I'm doing? I've been watching the course of the sun through the trees for two years, watching where it sets. In midsummer it sets there," he said, pointing to the tree framing the vista on the left, "so we'll only see the actual sunset in June, but we can enjoy the mountains and clouds and sky all year." He was giddy with excitement and pride. "I made this for you, darling, because I love you."

How he managed to figure out a way to expose this panorama by cutting down a minimum of trees and pruning a maximum of branches, all on our property, seemed a miracle. "See, you can see five peaks," and he named them off, left to right, "Overlook, Sugarloaf, Twin, Indian Head, Plattekill." He has climbed them all in winter, often alone with snowshoes or skis. I've never had the slightest urge to join him. "If you look closely, you can see the fire tower on the top of Overlook."

What a transformation! "You are not just an arborist," I told him, "you are an artist. Really, this is a classic Hudson Valley landscape scene!" The vista he had created and framed was more than worthy of a Thomas Cole painting. George was, in his own unique way, a Hudson River School artist: The landscape before him was his canvas; loppers, chainsaw, ladder, and rope, his tools.

All that winter, even when it was freezing and cloudy, George headed up to "the vista" every evening at sunset to gaze at the mountains. Sunset was early, before five, and I joined him only occasionally. Every morning George reported how many more minutes of sunlight we'd be treated to that day, as if it were his own doing.

On sunny mornings, he bundled up in layers and took his coffee there. I don't know what he thought about, if anything, as he stared out at the mountains. I had a bell that I rang when I wanted him to come back to the house, like the bell at the end of a meditation session.

The day before class began, an e-mail arrived from Professor Ben Stevens:

Dear Ovidians, Tomorrow we begin, in a sense, as Ovid ended: far from the city, in what may seem to be an excessively rural area, in what may seem to be blistering cold. This happy stance will help us to see more clearly certain things as Ovid did: from a sort of distance, with all the critical insight, irony, and complexity of inner experience such distance—spatial, temporal—can bring.

This seemed a propitious beginning. Most certainly I still felt an exile from my former life in the city. Even though it had now been four years since I'd moved away, my longing for the city was constant: a love I may never get over, a drug whose lure I may never entirely overcome. And god knows I could use some clarity on the past, which had so plagued me that autumn.

The Bard campus is a much shorter commute than Vassar, though it cannot compete with Vassar's classic splendor. Founded in 1860 as St. Stephen's College, it began as a theological college for Episcopal clergy. John Bard had donated the white brick Blithewood Manor mansion and the stone Chapel of the Holy Innocents, which were the oldest buildings on the campus. In the course of 150 years, the college metamorphosed into a nonsectarian coeducational liberal arts school, committed to progressive and classical education. It was the first college in the United States to give full academic credits for the creative and performing arts.

The mansion and the chapel are campus anomalies: Among them a hodgepodge of architectural styles has been constructed. Though several recent buildings were designed by world-renowned architects—the dorms, the science center, the Frank Gehry–designed performing arts center—all display their own vernacular and don't seem to converse with one another. Nevertheless, it is a school devoted to the arts, and a great cultural institution for our region, bringing dance, opera, music, literature, slices of New York City culture to us rustics; it's one of the primary attractions of our area for intelligent, sophisticated people, a country redoubt for burned-out New Yorkers such as myself.

Our class was given the "moon room" in Olin Hall—the nicest room on the top floor of a modern classroom building, with a large circular window at the apex of the roofline. Ben Stevens, a recent PhD from the University of Chicago, was young, extremely thin, and rather nerdy-looking, sporting a big smile and a polka-dot bow tie (why do classicists favor polka dots?). He was not what I'd expected: I'd heard rumors he was a lady's man. I'd later learn that he was also a choral singer, a yoga instructor, and a science-fiction enthusiast.

Ben handed out a syllabus, at the top of which was a quote from Ovid:

> *Forsitan et nostrum nomen miscebitur istis*
> *nec mea Lethaeis scripta dabuntur aquis . . .*

> And perhaps my name will be associated with theirs
> perhaps my writings will not be given over to the
>   waters of Lethe . . .

Ovid was the youngest of the great poets of Rome's golden age, a full generation younger than Catullus, half a generation younger than Horace and Virgil, so he had the anxiety, or in his case, the gift, of the influence of all three. His poetry has always been controversial even in his own day: Quintilian, the first rhetorician, said of him, *Nimium amator ingenii sui* (He is too captivated by his own genius), and the philosopher Seneca the Elder, who conceded that Ovid was the greatest wit of his time, nevertheless opined, *Nescit quod bene cessit reliquere* (He didn't know when to stop being witty). Ovid, he tells us, was fully aware of his faults, even held fast to them. Once three of Ovid's poet friends asked if they could remove three lines from his opus, which they believed were the most extravagant examples of his over-the-top style. Ovid assented, on the condition that he could pick three lines that were not to be removed under any circumstances. And, no surprise, the three lines picked by both sides were the same. Ovid was not about to kill his darlings.

Ovid has gone in and out of favor many times. When the Germans established classical scholarship as a modern pursuit, they dismissed Ovid as less significant than the other poets; his poems were considered by some scholars to be *nugae,* although others even then regarded him as the Roman Shakespeare. Recently he's come back into fashion once again, not only with classicists but also with popular novelists and poets. The past changes, fortune's wheel turns again, the future is overtaken by the latest past.

As with Horace, most of Ovid's work has made its way through the millennia to us. The most famous is *The Metamorphoses,* an epic of transformation, from the world's creation to the apotheosis of Augustus. But there are many more. Among them: *Amores* (Loves), *Ars Amatoria* (The Art of Love), *Remedia Amoris* (Remedies for Love), and oddest of the lot, *Medicamina Faciei Femineae* (Medications for Feminine Appearance—a manual on cosmetics for women).

There were six of us in the class, the same proportion of male to female as at Vassar—two women other than me. Molly was just like Siobhan, shy and pimply and always hiding behind her hair; Hannah was afflicted with what seemed to be Parkinson's or another disease of the nervous system, but her brain overrode her tics: She was sharp as a tack. There were three young men: Leo, a Leonardo DiCaprio look-alike; Guy, a Bert Lott type; and Mark, a typically thin, sweet Latinist. All were obviously cisgender, and every student, save me, came to class equipped with laptop or iPhone.

❧

Over the course of the semester, Ben frequently made excursions (from the Latin *excurro*, to run out) on various words. My favorite of his explanations was how *caelus* (sky) gave birth to *caeruleus* (blue). Here not only the diminutive -*ulus* is used but also a rhotacism, with the *l* becoming an *r* for ease of pronunciation. And how wonderful is it to think of everything blue being a "little sky." Blue has always been my favorite color.

Ben also stressed scansion. "You need to learn to hear the poetry, so for me, learning to read aloud is as important as translating." We began with *Amores* I, written in elegiac couplets.

Elegiac meter is composed of a hexameter line of six metric feet followed by a pentameter line of five metric feet. In elegiac meter a foot is either a dactyl, one long syllable (dum) followed by two short syllables (dit-ty) or a spondee, two long syllables (dum, dum).

But, of course, nothing in Latin is ever that simple. The pentameter line always includes an *ictus* (break) in the spondee in the middle of the line, whose mate—or second long syllable—doesn't appear until the end of the line.

Elegiac meter is expressed thus:

$$-\overline{uu}\ |-\overline{uu}\ |-\overline{uu}\ |-\overline{uu}\ |-\overline{uu}|--$$

$$-\overline{uu}\ |-\overline{uu}\ |-\ ||\ -\overline{uu}\ |-\overline{uu}|-$$

143

The hexameter line of most poems ends with dum dit-ty, dum dum (dactyl, spondee). The pentameter line always ends in dum dit-ty dum dit-ty dum (dactyl, dactyl, second half of spondee).

We quickly learned that like many things Latin and Roman, scansion was easiest figured out backwards, beginning with the final two feet of each line. Although we had read aloud some of Catullus' and Propertius' elegiac couplets a few short months ago, I had to relearn the meter and stamp out the *pedes* with my feet.

Ovid's was a new and dazzling poetic universe. In the first poem we read, *Amores* I.1, Ovid declares he was trying to write of arms and war (like Virgil, *Arma virumque cano*), but Cupid laughed at him, stole a metric foot, shot him with a love arrow, and now it's Cupid to whom Ovid's poetry is beholden (Cupid being a metonym for love). Ovid argues with Cupid that he is invading others' territories: He doesn't belong in Cupid's camp, he has neither boyfriend nor girlfriend—*longas compta puella comas* (a girl well arranged in respect to her long hair; remember the accusative of respect?). Nevertheless, he is burning with love: *uror, et in vacuo pectore regnat Amor* (I burn, and love reigns over my empty heart). Metaphorically, the poem describes the transition from heroic meter (dactylic hexameter) to elegiac couplet (the same except the second line lacks one foot) as a sly metaphor for the rising and falling of the male member: He's not as crude in his language as Catullus, but it's hard to miss his implications, with one line rising up (*surrexit*) then weakening (*attenuat nervos*) or subsiding (*residat*) in the next.

Ovid is playful, audacious, devilishly witty, even self-deprecating. His poetics remind me of a song by Chubby

Checker that has always accompanied feats of multilayered mastery in my mind: "Do You Love Me (Now That I Can Dance)." In the song Chubby calls out all he can now do: the Twist, the Shout, the Mashed Potato, the Jerk, the Fly, and the Watusi. I remember every one of them.

Ovid makes Latin dance, and he does so not only with rhythm and meter but also with internal rhyme, repetition, and visual effects that make each poem an act in a drama. By my count, he uses twelve different poetic devices in *Amores* I.1, a poem of thirty lines: metonomy, synecdoche, chiasmus, alliteration, assonance, anaphora, asyndeton, interlocked word order, hyperbaton, onomatopoeia, *tricolon crescens,* and word picture. Here are some lines from *Amores* I.1:

> *Quid, si praeripiat flavae Venus arma Minervae,*
> *ventilet accensas flava Minerva faces?*
> *Quis probet in silvis Cererem regnare iugosis,*
> *lege pharetratae virginis arva coli?*
> *Crinibus insignem quis acuta cuspide Phoebum*
> *instruat, Aoniam Marte movente lyram?*

> What if Venus stole the weapons of blond Minerva,
> would blond Minerva breathe the wedding
> torches to life?
> Who would approve Ceres reigning over the
> hilly woods
> or the arrow-bearing virgin having dominion
> over the planted fields?
> Who would instruct Apollo, famed for his curly
> locks, to wield the sharpened blade
> while Mars strummed the Aeonian lyre?

In the penultimate line of the poem, Ovid uses a device that for me is the *summum* of Latin poetry: The word picture.

Cingere litorea flaventia tempora myrto

Encircle your golden temples with shore-myrtle (or, as written, encircle of the shore golden temples with myrtle)

This most thrilling of all the Latin poetic devices surely deserves a better name than "word picture." In Latin, because word placement can be anywhere and sense is determined by the inflection, poets can do this magic trick that doesn't well lend itself to English. Thus the actual words "shore-myrtle" (*litorea myrto*) encircle the words "golden temples" (*flaventia tempora*). The chiasmic placement of the words enacts their meaning.

Another example from *Metamorphoses* I, where Cupid does the same love mischief to Apollo: *sagittifera prompsit duo tela pharetra* (takes from the arrow-bearing quiver two spears) or, as written, arrow-bearing takes out from two spears quiver, so the placement of the words, with the arrows (*duo tela*) surrounded by the quiver (*sagittifera pharetra*), enacts the placement of the arrows in the quiver.

Why does this most wonderful of poetic strategies not have a Greek name, or at least a Latin one? I asked Ben Stevens, but he did not know, so I e-mailed both Rob Brown and Curtis, but neither were aware of a formal term for it, other than "iconic" or the boring "word picture" or "Virgilian word picture" (since Virgil was the first to excel at this strategy). Unlike the other poetic devices, ancient critics didn't recognize it.

Might it better be called "visual onomatopoeia"? My research turned up the term "technopaegnia," which is a poem in the shape of what it's writing about, such as Lewis Carroll's poem in *Alice's Adventures in Wonderland* that begins "Fury said to a mouse," which is written in the shape of a mouse's tail. The Web also revealed the word "onomableva," for nouns that look like the thing they label, such as I, which looks like a standing person, bed, with its headboard and footboard, and awkward, with its awkward wkw. But further research revealed this to be a neologism, back-formed from the Greek for word and resemble.

I'd like to coin an appropriate Latin term for a word picture. Perhaps *verba acta* (words enacted) or *verba imaginata* (words in image) or *imago in verbis* (image in words)?

I asked my friend Jan Heller Levi, an accomplished poet, if there's anyone who can do this in English. A few days later, this excerpt from an E. E. Cummings poem arrived via e-mail:

> somewhere I have never travelled, gladly beyond
> any experience, your eyes have their silence:
> in your most frail gesture are things which enclose me,
> or which I cannot touch because they are too near
>
> your slightest look easily will unclose me
> though I have closed myself as fingers,
> you open always petal by petal myself as Spring opens
> (touching skilfully, mysteriously) her first rose
>
> —E. E. Cummings

The last two lines come as close as English can get, with the *petal by petal* slowly revealing *myself.* I had always loved E. E.

Cummings when I was in high school, and later, as I was recovering from breast cancer, his poem "i thank You God for most this amazing day" was my prayer. In the depths of chemo, staring down death, every day of being alive was a blessing. Like Ovid, E. E. Cummings has gone in and out of fashion; recently he's come back in. He was, of course, a Latinist.

As we proceeded on to selections of the *Metamorphoses,* Ovid's visual acuity with words was well in evidence. In *Pyramus and Thisbe* (IV.121–24), he has a bloody description worthy of Quentin Tarantino, written, I suspect, with equal wryness:

> *Cruor emicat alte,*
> *non aliter quam cum vitiato fistula plumbo*
> *scinditur et tenui stridente foramine longas*
> *eiaculatur aquas atque ictibus aera rumpit.*

> Blood spurted up high,
> not unlike when a faulty lead pipe is split open,
> and shoots out long streams of water
> from a small hissing opening,
> and burst in jets into the air.

Here's a more pleasing example: In *Metamorphoses* V.592–96, Arethusa, a wood nymph, tells her story. Always embarrassed by her beauty, and not desiring to please men, she was a fine hunter and wanderer in mountain meadows. One hot day she came upon a lovely clear stream. She then describes, in seductive imagery, what is almost a striptease, as she cools herself in the stream. Here Ovid puts us in the gaze of Alpheus, the river god down below, as Arethusa tells her tale:

Accessi, primumque pedis vestigia tinxi,
poplite deinde tenus; neque eo contenta, recingor,
molliaque inpono salici velamina curvae,
nudaque mergor aquis; quas dum ferioque trahoque
mille modis labens, excussaque bracchia iacto

I approached, and first dipped in the tips of my feet
then as far as my knees; not content with that, I strip off
my soft robes and hang them from a curving willow
and naked I merge with the waters. While I strike
    and stroke the water
gliding in a thousand ways I flourish and shake
    my arms

If she's so chaste, why such a description, we might ask? Is not Ovid once again enacting a sexual metaphor? Does this not sound like foreplay?

Arethusa does disturb and excite the river god Alpheus, who exhorts her to stay, but she runs all the way to Diana, who hides her in a fine mist. As Alpheus, momentarily taking bodily form, stares at the mist, she gradually liquefies. Alpheus returns to his river form, hoping their fluids might mingle, but Diana sinks Arethusa down deep underground, whence she rises up into the air as a fountain.

                  ❧

At our last class before the two-week March break, Ben Stevens finally had some words to say about the incursion of the computer in our classroom. "For the next part of class, I'm going to ask you all not to bring your computers; they're a distraction."

I admired Ben's tact. Leonardo frequently read his translations from a cell phone. Were they downloaded from elsewhere on the Internet or had he translated them himself and keyed them in on that tiny keyboard? There was no way to know. And Guy, with his laptop ever at the ready to look up a word in class, was just as often surfing the Internet and shopping when it wasn't his turn to translate. I knew because I sat next to him.

During the break, I read all of *The Metamorphoses*, getting up from time to time to stare out the window and gaze at the mostly barren landscape that surrounded me. When I lived in New York City, I'd spend hours on my window seat overlooking Riverside Drive, watching the people parade pass by. I could tell the weather by their dress: light or heavy coats, necks naked or wrapped with scarves. I liked charting the change of season through the intermittent splashes of color that enlivened the drab black, brown, and grey winter coats.

Here I have only squirrel, deer, and birds to watch. Though Ovid tells of no human being changed into a squirrel, legions (over forty by my count) are turned into birds in *The Metamorphoses*, a few of which are named: crow, hawk, dove, stork, heron, owl, eagle, magpie, and woodpecker. Of those, many have made their way onto our property to use our bird feeder and suet; luckily, some stay all winter long.

The kitchen and living-room windows look directly out onto a stone patio, behind which stands a small magnolia tree swathed in a petticoat of deer netting. A bird feeder hangs from its highest branch. On the other side of the patio, a bright blue bluebird box sits atop a rusty, six-foot pole, a suet cage dangling from it like an outsized earring. That patio is the metropolitan hub of our yard. Birds come and go all day, particularly in the morning—juncos, chickadees, and a pair of cardinals, dazzling splashes of red in the brown, grey, and white winter landscape. In February a pair of red-bellied woodpeckers arrives. Why they are called red-bellied is a mystery—there's no discernable red or even a blush of rose on their bellies. The male sports a full red Mohawk, the female a mere yarmulke of red. The doves, who are ground feeders, also arrive in February. But I always have my eyes peeled for bluebirds, my favorite harbingers of spring, who arrive even before the robins.

My first father-in-law used to say that if you want to understand human society, raise chickens. I've now come to think the same is true for all birds; I can watch them for hours. There are alphas, betas, aggressives and passives, and those who avoid the pecking order altogether, just as there are in human society. The male woodpecker chases a junco from the feeder to the less favored suet, where the junco flaps and flutters and drives away his cousin or wife, whoever got there first. As soon as the woodpecker flies off, the juncos return to the feeder. The doves stay on the ground, where they avoid conflict and enjoy dropped seed.

In *The Metamorphoses,* most of the humans are turned into birds for failing to love the god or goddess who desires them. The saddest of all, for me, is *Picus,* the handsome prince of Latium who spurns Circe, the weaver goddess of magic, because he so loves his wife, *Canens* (Singing). Circe does not like being denied, and as *Picus* rushes back to his wife, she turns him into a woodpecker. His powerful beak knocks against trunks and branches in perpetual anger and frustration. His wife, whom Circe holds equally responsible, is turned into nothing but air. We have our own *Picus* here in the summers, a magnificent pileated woodpecker, whose slow, powerful drumming we begin hearing in the early spring, and whose deep *kuk kuk kuk* echoes through the forest.

I hope, if I'm turned into a bird, I might be a bluebird, or perhaps an owl, like the barred owl whose plangent *hooo hooo hoo hooooooo (who cooks for youuuuu:* a spondee and an iamb) we hear on summer nights, sometimes echoing another call in the distance. But I fear I might be a hummingbird, whose fast machinelike whir announces its arrival even before you see it. Like me, it is always in motion. George would certainly be an eagle, sitting up high somewhere, watching the world below.

By the time class ends in May, the bluebirds have built their nest in the birdhouse, the doves are feeding on the seed they've dropped to the ground, the robins have arrived with their warbling song, and George has found yet another vista he's been seeking for several years. He has attended several presentations given by Michael Kudish, a retired professor of environmental science and forestry who has devoted his life to studying the history of the Catskill forests. He also has taken several educational forest walks offered by Kudish. Last winter he returned from a day's outing to report that there was a Latinist among Kudish's acolytes. "He wanders off on his own and finds plants to show us," George told me. "And he knows all the Latin names for them. I think he must have a photographic memory. You should come to one of these outings and meet him." That seemed unlikely.

George was now hunting for a trail Kudish himself knew existed but had never found, a carriage trail that led from the lower slopes of Mount Tremper to the vista at the top. Armed with his geological survey maps, he was determined to find it. The Zen Mountain Monastery, at which George is a sometimes student, sits at the base of that mountain, and George has come to feel a special affinity with it. As I have favorite words (-ids, -ims, et cetera), George has favorite mountains.

In the 1800s, New Yorkers fled the heat and humidity of the city and summered in the Catskills. Some of them stayed in the grand hotels that were scattered all over the mountaintops. With the advent of air-conditioning, the hotels fell into desuetude and finally burned down. Only one, the Mohonk Mountain House, still stands. Most were built at a high elevation, where spectacular views of the range were only a short walk from the hotel. One of the hotels, on Mount Tremper, was situated in a valley; from it, guests were transported to view the mountaintop panorama via horse and carriage, not unlike George and I, who must travel an uphill trail to enjoy our vista. George follows several types of trails. In descending order of width they are: carriage trails, quarry roads used to transport bluestone, bark roads for transporting the hemlock bark used in tanning, bridal paths for horses, and hiking paths for people.

After several unsuccessful forays on the mountain, George finally found what he was looking for: an old carriage trail that went halfway up the mountain on a well-graded, if abandoned, road. But it soon petered out to a barely discernable path. That's when George discovered an unusual guide: Bobcat tracks in the snow led him up and up to the top of the mountain. "I never saw the bobcat," he later told me, "but I definitely had the sense he was leading me to the summit."

George studies old trails the way I study old language, taking off on various roads (authors) and tangents (poetic lines). For him the different characteristics of trails are as interesting as the sequence of tenses is for me: He is visual, I am verbal. How different he is than the other men I've loved. Month by month, year by year, I'm learning to accept, even delight in, our differences. He gives me a kind of love and comfort no man ever has before. I now look elsewhere for conversation about books and words—especially New York. In my younger years, I required sophistication in the men I loved; now all I ask for is kindness.

That's a transformation age allows, along with the happy triangle I enjoy every June, when both my straight and gay "husbands" are in residence. Once again, the house gets a thorough Steve cleaning, and I have a chattering mate to keep me company while I garden. That year, partly in celebration of Steve, I had a rose trellis built on the wall between the house and barn, and by the time Steve left at the beginning of July, a red floribunda rose was climbing around on it, surrounded by Russian sage and the foliage of the dinner-plate dahlias I'd planted for late-summer glory. Because it's a narrow, triangular-shaped garden between the wall of the barn and the wall of the house, I figured it would be safe for roses: surely the deer won't want to hazard the narrow bluestone trail I'd laid to bisect the garden. I wanted to attract my kindred busy hummingbirds, who love red flowers, and here, I hoped, they would not act as nymphs, luring the deer gods, at whose pleasure my gardens thrived or were destroyed.

CHAPTER 10

Si hortum in biblioteca habes, deerit nihil.

If you have a garden in your library, you will lack nothing.

—Cicero

With the cool, clearing light of September, class began again, and none too soon. By August, I had despaired of my newly planted rose garden. Despite my efforts to foil them, the deer had eaten every single bloom on my otherwise flourishing roses. My dinner-plate dahlias were nipped in the bud; even the "deer-proof" perennials—bee balm and cupid's dart—in my other gardens had been decimated. Decimate comes from the Latin verb *decimare* and means "to select one in ten for punishment." In English, the meaning of the word has changed over the years. The *American Heritage Dictionary* defines decimate as: "1. To destroy or kill a large part of (a group). 2. To inflict great destruction or damage on: as in the fawns decimated my rose bushes." At least English got the result right, if not the primary meaning.

Ought a proper Latinist eschew the modern mutations of Latin word meanings? Should I say, "By September, the deer were so ravenous they left only the grey-foliaged plants untouched"? Who needed this reminder of age (*canities*)? My hair was grey and so was my dog, Augie, now older than I in dog years. And I was already dreading the grey of the coming winter. Grey needs color to brighten it, like cardinals in winter. So I bought a new, bright-red lipstick. It accentuated my blue eyes and silver hair like the roses and delphiniums might have accented my artemisia and lamb's ear had deer not devoured my flowers.

I was returning to Vassar for fall semester and looking forward to seeing my old teachers and classmates. I dressed for class that first fall day in lavender, put on my makeup so as not to alarm whatever new youths might be my classmates, and finished myself off by applying my new lipstick. Early, as always, I headed to the Retreat for breakfast and, just as I opened the door, there was Curtis, walking out with a giant cup of soda pop.

"Now you're sure you don't want to learn Greek with me?" he said. "Last chance!" It was the only class he was teaching, and he still didn't know where he'd be next year, whether at Vassar or landing a new job elsewhere.

I wanted to take Greek and longed to take another class with Curtis, but I was afraid I would lose all my Latin if I tried. Not to mention, I felt I needed at least five more years of Latin before I was anywhere near proficient. We had a nice chat, and at the end he put on a more serious look, touched my arm, and said, "Now, Ann, we're friends, aren't we?"

I was alarmed. "I hope so," I said.

"This might not be my place," he said, "and I hope you don't mind my saying this, but you have lipstick on your teeth." I thanked him profusely and assured him that he was, indeed, a good friend, *bonus amicus,* then ran to the nearest ladies' room. Was I becoming more and more eccentric, no longer the glamorous, high-powered publisher, merely an oldster auditor who couldn't even get her lipstick on straight?

That semester I was taking two classes, Roman Epigraphy and Roman History, both taught by Bert Lott. Earlier, I had visited him to ask for permission to take both, wondering if that might seem too greedy. "Not at all," he said, but he warned me that he would be "very professor-y" in the history class, maybe not as fun as he had been in the seminar. "You'll have to listen to me talk even more than usual," he joked.

"I'll enjoy that," I assured him. "I'll have a semester of a lot of Lott!"

After three years of study, I was eager to learn more of the Roman history I'd picked up in disconnected dribs and drabs from studying poetry and listening to novels about Rome by Steven Saylor, Robert Harris, and Colleen McCullough as I drove in my car. It made the daily commute seem more useful.

The epigraphy class was held in the same large room as Beginning Latin, a comparatively big class: eight students! Alissa was back from her junior year abroad in Italy—she had metamorphosed into a young woman: more confident, more attractive, and more grown-up in every way. Naftali was a familiar junior, and now there was Peter, a senior, who sported purple and red polished nails, and Xavier, who had a full head of long, stringy brown hair, which he inexplicably wore in something resembling a comb-over. There were two new women: redheaded Sharon, a shy junior, and Gita, a freshman from a New York City private school. The only Latin student at Vassar who always brought her computer to class, Gita was habitually late and the class usually waited and watched as she removed the computer from her brightly patterned backpack, turned it on, and finally sat down. She never brought a book, but, like a court reporter, typed on the computer constantly throughout class. Correcting her translations? Writing down everything Bert Lott said? I never could tell. She was noticeably more self-confident than anyone else in the room, though not the best Latinist among us.

Last to arrive was Siddhi, a slightly Goth, gorgeous young man sporting long brown hair, lavender wifebeater T-shirt, low-slung black jeans complete with key chain leading from belt loop to back pocket, two leather necklaces, three bracelets, four rings—and radiating sex. *Ecastor!!!* Not your typical Latin scholar, to be sure.

He sat next to Alissa, and the two immediately begin chatting. It turned out they were roommates. How was it this young woman was always with the cutest boy in the room? Was Siddhi straight or gay? I couldn't tell, but he was captivating, very friendly, and very sweet. And what sort of name was Siddhi? And why did Xavier refer to him as Justin? Ralph and Peter, both of whom were clearly gay, entered the conversation from the other side of the room, and soon everyone in the class was chattering.

Bert Lott, the leader of the pack, entered to enthusiastic *Salves!* Bert is an epigrapher first and foremost and contagiously in love with his subject. He was sometimes almost giddy with excitement as he introduced what he hoped to accomplish during the semester. The class was nothing like a regular Latin class, more like a treasure hunt, with Bert leading our very enthusiastic crew in ferreting out stories from stones.

As Bert laid out the syllabus, Siddhi kept pumping his arm in the air saying, "Cool, cool."

"I don't know how this is going to go," Bert warned us, "I may have to throw this syllabus out altogether, it depends how much trouble we all have coming to terms with these inscriptions. The last time I did this, I took the class out to the Vassar cemetery so we could study modern inscriptions, but we were not too kindly asked to leave. I was told I was being disrespectful to the dead, though I don't really think they minded at all. In fact, I believe they enjoyed our company and interest."

The Romans had what scholars call "the epigraphic habit," especially during the reign of Augustus. "Augustus loved to see his name and accomplishments written in stone. He was the first of the Roman emperors, and he made sure no one forgot it," Bert mused. There are over half a million Latin inscriptions, some on bronze, most on stone, that have survived the millennia. Back in the beginning of the twentieth century, Bert told us, Vassar had a first-rate classical archaeology department, as well as a classical museum, which was consolidated with the current Lehman Loeb Art Center in the seventies.

Also around that time, fourteen inscribed marbles "somehow made their way back to Vassar"; it was more or less legal to bring home such souvenirs (viz., the Elgin Marbles and the current battles raging about important antiquities being returned to the countries from which they were plundered). No one knows who the collector was. The fourteen marbles were plastered into the walls of the Vassar Classical Museum until they were finally removed and stored in the basement of the Lehman Loeb Art Center, where, Bert told us, "they have been sitting uncatalogued, unresearched, untranslated, and unloved ever since."

It would be our task, at the beginning of the semester, to edit and catalogue these inscriptions so they could be added to the master list of Roman inscriptions: the *Corpus Inscriptionum Latinarum,* commonly referred to as the *CIL.* Editing an inscription involves deciphering it in Latin, trying to date it, identifying those named on it, and guessing what purpose it served. Inscriptions so studied include laws, road signs, calendars, Senate decrees, and, most commonly, grave epitaphs and other forms of memorials. Each of us would be assigned two stones to edit, which left me, an auditor, without stones. Luckily, Alissa had a schedule change and had to drop the class, thus leaving her two stones to me.

After class, I visited Curtis at his office, and we discussed the students in the class.

"And there are two longhairs, Xavier and Siddhi," I said. "They're already my favorites."

He shook his head. "Of course," he said. "Ever the Berkeley girl."

Xavier, he explained, was a Greek specialist, and flat-out brilliant. "Straight or gay?" I asked. No one knew. "And hottie Siddhi," I said, "what about him?"

"Ah, Justin," Curtis said. "He's the Latin intern this year."

"So what's his name? Justin or Siddhi?"

Curtis gave his winning wry smile. "Actually it's Siddhartha," he said, "though he doesn't always use that name. His parents are old hippies, probably like you, and it's some kind of name he chose or something, I'm not sure."

Siddhartha! Could anyone be more appealing? I would later learn, from Siddhi himself, that his parents were members of the SYDA Foundation. Brahmins of Siddha Yoga had bestowed the name on him, the equivalent of a baptism. He preferred Siddhartha to Justin. Another boon of my age, I can fall in love with young people with no heat behind it, nothing but a pure enjoyment of their youth and a feeling of benevolence toward them. And isn't that what I really want my life to be now, enjoyment and benevolence?

As I would every Tuesday and Thursday, I passed the three and a half hours between classes eating lunch, studying in the library, sometimes taking a walk, and sometimes reading in the Victorian "Rose Room" above the student center. The Rose Room was the parlor of the original college building, a large, gracious room with mirrored columns and oversized windows, furnished with Victorian couches, lamps, and a grand piano. A marble staircase and mirrored hallway lead to it. Both were built extra wide to accommodate the hooped skirts women wore at the founding of the college in the 1860s. Now and again a few students would take their lunch there. Once a beautiful soprano accompanied herself on the piano for a song or two. Usually I was there alone.

The Roman History class was altogether different. It was held in a large lecture hall in the modern, unattractive science building. Only three other Latinists, Sharon, Peter, and Naftali, were enrolled. Peter and I sat together, with both Sharon and Naftali flanking us—a nucleus with two electrons. Bert was a great lecturer, with his big personality and self-confessed love of his own cleverness, his wonderful way of making Roman motivations seem like a contemporary reality show. Bert's seventy-five-minute classes were like professorial performance art: Irreverent, sardonic, he mixed ancient history with commentary in up-to-the-minute slang. We were constantly amused as he sped us through six hundred years of Roman history in twenty-six short lessons.

"I love to hear myself talk," he warned the class of twenty-eight students. "I expect you to come to class prepared so you don't have to listen to me all the time. You cannot interrupt other students, but I'll always be happy if you interrupt me."

Bert was never interrupted in Roman History class. He'd arrive every day and greet us enthusiastically, "Hi, how is everybody today?" and be met, every day, with a wall of silence. Whenever he asked a question in class, he usually answered it himself, having tired of waiting for a raised hand. The opposite was true of the epigraphy class, where each of the seven of us asked questions, ventured guesses, laughed at Bert's jokes, and parried with our own.

We met in the library for the second epigraphy class, and Bert took us on a tour of the research books we would be using. The Roman section was downstairs in the stacks. The *CIL Romanum* comprised six gigantic, much-repaired volumes that catalogue every known inscription found in Rome. It was the first time I had seen the historian's arcana. It was awesome, which word I use in its proper sense to mean awe inspriring, not as it is now so commonly misused to mean good or simply okay.

For the third class we met in a seminar room in the art museum. We were asked to leave all of our possessions in lockers before we entered the room where the fourteen stones were laid out on thick white paper atop a long table. We were each given a pair of spanking-clean white gloves, the sort used by film editors, to protect the stones from the depredations of human touch.

What a thrill it was to be able to handle those ancient stones, to anticipate deciphering their language! By the end of the eighty minutes, we had each chosen two stones, carefully measured them in centimeters, written down the letters inscribed there, and catalogued any decorative features. "These will become your stones for the semester," Bert told us, "and you'll get to know them intimately. After today they'll be displayed in the front hallway here, so you can visit your stones and commune with them whenever you like. But you won't be able to touch them ever again."

All were funerary stones.

❧

Though a study in contrasts, the two classes were perfect companions: Epigraphy was the raw material of history, an artifactual reminder that much of ancient history is "history from square brackets." In epigraphy, as in literature, square brackets are used to indicate guesses the editor has made about letters, words, or entire phrases that are missing on a stone or in a manuscript—what has been worn away by time, weather, or erasure, or where a piece has been broken off and remains unfound. From their own deep knowledge and references from other sources, epigraphers make educated guesses to reconstruct history and add missing words, which are placed in [square brackets].

Because so much knowledge of history is gained from epigraphs, as well as from the historical texts that were copied over the years, epigraphy can and often has changed the past when and if those square brackets get filled in.

Over the last two decades, many bronzes have been found in a region of southeastern Spain. With the advent of personal metal detectors in the 1990s, Spanish farmers began hunting for inscribed tablets in their fields, selling their finds to antiquities dealers who in turn sold them to museums or universities. Bronzes are particularly prized because so many of them had been melted down for other uses, bronze being as dear then as it is now. Six copies on bronze of a much-attested decree condemning Gnaeus Calpurnius Piso during the time of Tiberius were found in the same area of Spain. Historians knew of the decree because Tacitus wrote about it extensively. However, the actual decree inscribed on the newly discovered bronzes revealed that Tacitus had more than freely interpreted the event to serve his own historical bias. The discoveries changed the way historians read Tacitus. Kofi Busia's mantra, "You can only change the past," rings out again.

Our history class was filled with references to epigraphy. The first recorded legal document we have from Rome is known as the Twelve Tables. They are believed to have been made around 449 B.C., were inscribed on both stone and bronze, and were posted publicly all over Rome so every Roman could read and know them. The Twelve Tables remained the basis of Roman law for centuries and heavily influenced our own constitution and jurisprudence. The Twelve Tables codified the legal and civil rights of patricians and plebeians, established procedures for courts and trials, and delineated both public and sacred law: the payments of debts, return of loaned property, rights of land and possession, remedies for bodily injury and defamation, inheritance laws, and guardianship.

One entire section was devoted to the rights of fathers over the family, which included a father's right to kill his son, as well as his obligation to kill a badly deformed child.

Marriage between a patrician and a plebeian was forbidden.

If a man and woman lived together for an entire year without an interruption of three or more nights, she "passed into his power" as his legal wife, which meant she was legally treated as the man's daughter.

If a husband desired to divorce his wife, he had only to give a reason for doing so.

The laws also required women to refrain from tearing at their faces or scratching their cheeks with their nails during a funeral, or making loud cries of mourning for the dead.

If any person publicly abused another in a loud voice, or wrote a poem that insulted or rendered him infamous, he was beaten with a rod until death.

Unlike the powerless female "whom our ancestors believed, by reason of levity of disposition," should remain in guardianship regardless of age, the poet (masculine first-declension noun) was taken seriously.

Anyone who used incantations or magic to prevent crops from growing, or who used any magic arts to render another person ill, was punished with death.

In the early days of Rome, writing and the alphabet were

considered the ingredients of magic. Lott told us that curses on rivals, engraved on lead tablets and rolled and struck through with a blade, have been found at the bottom of ancient wells. In those days, writing had the power to make the ephemeral real: *abracadabra,* the magical incantation still used to pull rabbits out of hats, is all about the ABCs. In the Middle Ages, there was a German sect known as the Abecedarians who eschewed the written word entirely. All truths, they believed, came directly from god in visions or in ecstatic states, and human learning only got in the way of God's truth. They believed that one must be ignorant of even the first letters of the alphabet if one were to be saved; hence the name, ABCdarians. They're still alive and well, under other nomenclature: creationists, climate change deniers, Fox News watchers, much of the Republican Party.

Peter emerged as the best student in the epigraphy class and was always asking the subtle question or raising an interesting possibility. And like me, he always arrived early. It must be a midwestern thing. Peter, like me, was born in Indiana and would be going to law school the following year. He had already taken six seminars in advanced Latin and worried he would miss it in law school. He often wore scarves, three different and fabulous scarves that a friend had knit or crocheted for him. I spent one class examining the pattern on his crocheted scarf, which turned out to be simple, worked it up, and we soon had twin scarves: mine blue, his green. I almost brought my crocheting to class but then thought better of it. I wonder if my retention of vocabulary would improve if I crocheted while listening. Would the kinesthetic motion help fix it in my brain, or would its distraction obviate the salubrious effects? The fates wove people's story lines in Roman times; I was weaving mine with words, which are, in their own way, the garment I wear.

My stones:

C NONIUS.

C L SALVIUS

Gaius Nonius Salvius, Freedman of Gaius

D M

VALENTINO.FILI

O. QUI VIXIT. ANV

MES.V.AVR.ACH

ILLES M. CHO.VIII P

PATER FECIT DULC

ISSIMO. B.M. FECIT

To the Gods of the Shades
For his sweetest son Valentinus
who lived five years, five months,
his father, Aurius Achilles,
soldier of the eighth Praetorian Cohort made it.
For his well deserving son he made it.

＊

As we were working on editing our stones, Bert assigned other inscriptions for study and translation: epitaphs, inscriptions on buildings, infrastructure (yes, even aqueducts and bridges were inscribed!), honorifics, and religious inscriptions. Rome allowed many gods—household gods neighborhood gods, and city gods—until near the end of the empire when Christianity overtook not only the gods but also the Roman Empire. The only religious practice ever outlawed in early Rome was the Bacchanalias, imported from the Dionysian Cult Mysteries of Greece. The ceremonies included liberal use of intoxicants and trance-inducing dance and music. Rumors of sexual orgies were rife. Most believe Bacchanalias were singled out because the cult was largely composed of women running wild, and one thing nearly every Roman senator believed was that it was essential to keep women in line.

Spending so much time with Roman history made my feminist rage burgeon anew. I kept thinking about my mother, my powerless mother, and all those women who were so powerless for so many centuries, under the control of husbands. It was the gift of the feminist movement in my formative years that allowed me to focus on earning my own way and being independent. Unlike my mother, I did not choose men who might dominate me. I wanted to be in charge.

For homework Bert assigned us his commentary on one of the inscriptions: a decree by the town council of Pisa outlining commemorative honors to be made to Lucius Caesar. "Some hack wrote this," he said as he handed it out.

And what should I find in his commentary on this inscription but the word "epexegetic," which obscure favorite I had learned from Curtis the year before and imagined I would never see again. In Lott's commentary it is not an infinitive that is epexegetic but a conjunction: *que*, which placed on the end of a word is to be read as "and" before that word:

> In the line *inferiae mittantur bosque et ovis atri* (sacrifices should be sent: a black cow and a black sheep) the *que* in *bosque* (bull) is epexegetic, in this case explaining just what specific infernal offerings were to be made, rather than copulative, which would be translated to mean that *inferiae* (sacrifices) as well as a bull and a black sheep (*ovis atri*) were offered. The epexegetic *que* tells us that the bull and sheep are

the *inferiae*. Thus, "et" is used between them to denote a simpler "and."

So a conjunction can be exepegetic as well as copulative!

Though Bert is a supremely supple Latinist, we didn't do a lot of translating that semester. Most of my memorization was learning the many abbreviations used in inscriptions: the most common *D M* (*Dis Manibus,* to the sacred shades), *L* (*libertus,* freedman), *F* (*filius,* son), and the true kicker, *Q D E R F P D E R I C* (*Quid de ea re fieri placeret de ea re ita censuerunt,* it was decided what concerning this matter will be pleasing to be done about this matter). Latin, that most concise of languages, was redundant in legalese.

As we spent three weeks going over our edited stones each day, the interest in our class turned almost to exhilaration. None of us had done a perfect job editing our stones, but Lott was happy to fill in the blanks, demonstrating the questions each letter might lead you to ask and what databases you might use to search for answers. He showed how one thing led to another. Just as I search out the meanings of words, he searches out the meanings of letters, enacting for us his historical method or, as he called it, "going hunting."

For example, freed slaves were always referred to by *L* (for *libertus*) and then their owner's name, as in *C L* on my first stone above. If the owner was a woman, a backwards *C* was used to represent her. Bert's explanation: Since *Caius* (Gaius) was the most common *praenomen,* all the epigraphers were good at *C*'s, so they figured they'd just write it backwards for a woman. My feminist ire boils again. This symbol disappeared during the second century A.D., by which time most women were given their own *praenomina,* rather than simply the feminine version of their father's praenomen. The trend started only in the mid-first century, with the power of Livia Augustus. I think again of my mother with her many names and her rage when she shouted, "Just call me shit." I had committed the sin of reminding her that she didn't even have her own name.

We also learned some tricks for dating. If an inscription contains the letters Ⅎ or Ⅎ we can date it to Claudius' reign. Claudius felt it essential to create these new letters, the Ⅎ to represent the consonantal *U* (*W* and *V* hadn't yet been invented) and the Ⅎ to represent the Greek *Υ*, which hadn't yet been absorbed into the Latin alphabet. (*Υ* was the last letter to join the Latin alphabet, preceded by *J* and *W* and *V*.) Claudius also invented a third letter, but since no inscription bearing it has been found, we don't know what it looked like. We know all this from mentions by Tacitus and from Suetonius, who tells us:

> Claudius invented three new letters which he added to the alphabet. These he believed were urgently needed. He published a book about them before becoming emperor, and afterward put them into general use. These characters may still be seen in books, in official registers, and in inscriptions on public buildings dating from that period.

After Claudius' death, the letters were never used again.

The history class revealed yet another change the present has made on the past. In my day, eras were dated B.C. (Before Christ) and A.D. (*Anno Domini,* in the year of our lord). In the early years of the PC seventies, historians began using a new nomenclature that pushed Jesus out of the calendar in recognition of the non-Christian portion of the world. B.C. became B.C.E., before the Common Era, and A.D. became C.E., Common Era.

The expression "Common Era" comes from the Latin *vulgaris aera* (*vulgaris* means "ordinary" or "common," not the crass or crude display that "vulgar" has evolved into today). Since my days in college, which ended in 1974, C.E. and B.C.E. have taken over. The abbreviations can be used to mean whatever the writer wants, the C doing double duty as either Christian or Common. Nevertheless, because he was outraged that Wikipedia used only C.E. and B.C.E., the Christian fundamentalist Andrew Schlafly, son of Phyllis Schlafly (she who campaigned against the Equal Rights Amendment and modern feminism), created Conservapedia, a wiki encyclopedia created to counter the "liberal bias" of Wikipedia. It, of course, uses only B.C. and A.D.

I presented my second stone, which Bert had warned me was the most difficult of the fourteen to edit, with as many questions as assertions. Bert enthusiastically told us that he had figured out the stone, had even found it in *CIL*. Watching Bert talking about his solution was like watching a prospector report on his discovery of a valuable gold mine. The *M* stood for *miles* (soldier). The *P* was a symbol for the Praetorian Guards, and *Cho* the abbreviation for "Cohort," two things I never could have figured out on my own.

After the semester break each of us would be given an entire seventy-five-minute class to present the long inscription we had chosen out of a list Bert had given us. I chose my inscription last, feeling it was only right, since I wasn't a paying customer, and got for my project the *Laudatio Turiae* (In praise of Turia), which I had wanted anyway. It was the only inscription among the ten that was for a woman. As the sign-up sheet for the date of our presentation made its way around, I was also last to choose. Predictably I would be the first to present after break, as the other students wanted the extra weeks to prepare.

I spent hours in the library, researching, reading commentaries, delving more deeply into the world of Roman historians. My feminist outrage grew by the week. How lucky I was to be born at the time I was. What would have become of me if I'd been part of my mother's generation? What might she have become if she'd had the choices I had? Wouldn't she have loved to do what I was doing now? Wouldn't this have provided her, as it was providing me, a pursuit more fulfilling than crossword puzzles? Might it even have kept her alive?

CHAPTER 11

It is astonishing how much enjoyment one can get out of
a language that one understands imperfectly.

—Basil Gildersleeve

During semester break, I visited an inspiring after-
school program my friend Patrick introduced me to,
at which local Hispanic kids, in the still-ungentrified
regions of Bushwick, Brooklyn, studied Latin on Wednesday
afternoons. The free program, Still Waters in a Storm, gives
kids homework help five days a week, and after homework is
done, at 5:00 P.M., violin, yoga, and Latin are offered on various days. On weekends well-known writers come to give the
kids writing workshops. I contacted the director, Stephen Haff,
and asked if he'd like another Latin tutor. He was most welcom-
ing. The very next Wednesday I traveled to Bushwick, where I'd
never been, to a storefront that housed Still Waters in a Storm.

The classroom, a controlled chaos of opportunity, was
unlike any other I've ever seen: There were long walls of bookshelves festooned with Tibetan prayer flags and colored Christmas lights. Above a white piano was a bright Picasso print of a
blue and yellow cubist man, and a chalkboard on which was
written *Salve!* as well as the conjugation of *amo, amare.* Books

and pictures, notebooks and artwork were stacked in piles on the floor. A string of tables stood in the center of the room, where kids from six to twelve were working on various projects. Others leaned into one another over books on couches. At the back in a small alcove was a table where pizza (*laganum,* literally "a cake of flour and oil") was served at 5:00.

Stephen, with four or five kids hanging on him waiting for the turn of his attention, welcomed me warmly. He is a somewhat shaggy man in his early forties, his blond-grey hair tousled, a two-day stubble on his chin, his glasses askew. Like Mister Rogers, he wore a plaid shirt and a blue cardigan, and he exuded a similar aura of a gentle kindness. Suddenly there was commotion, running and shouting, and Stephen stood up, clapped his hands, and said, "It's getting too loud and boisterous in here. Everyone is working on different things, and we have to respect our friends' work and be quiet enough so everyone can concentrate." On a dime, the running stopped, the shouting stopped, and everyone turned back to whatever task was at hand.

Stephen refers to Still Waters as a sanctuary for children. His model for his one-room schoolhouse is Alcoholics Anonymous and Quaker meetings, and his guiding principles are listening, learning, and imagination, and, encompassing everything he does, is love. Not only does Stephen provide a safe place for the children to express their feelings by writing and responding to others, he also teaches them to listen with attention and empathy. It's a two-way street: What a child has to express is as important as what an adult expresses. There are no cliques here, no insiders and outsiders, only a group of thirty kids who respect and help one another.

Since most of the kids are Spanish speaking, Stephen

realized in the third year of his program that he could put his proficiency in Latin to good use. "Our language is our identity," he said, "and learning Latin gives our kids pride in their heritage. It's much easier to learn Latin if you're a native Spanish speaker, and the kids love it; it makes them feel special."

Stephen told me the Latinists were working on translating *Olivia Porca* (*Olivia the Pig*) and, without further instruction, led me to a round table in one corner and introduced me to two nine-year-olds, Kimberly and Maya, who had already translated some of the short picture book and were eager for more. Maya looked two years older than Kimberly, and as soon as I sat down, she put her copy of the book in Latin before me. She'd written her translation above the Latin words, just as I do when I translate poetry. "See," she said, "I'm ahead of all the others, I'm almost finished, and I really need to finish first so we have to do it today." I asked her if it was really that important that she finish first, and told her I didn't think it was. "Oh, it is," she repeated. "Believe me, it is very important."

Another driven girl! I immediately loved her. "What sign are you?" I asked. And sure enough, she, too, is an Aries (and as Curtis was happy to tell me, Aries means not only "ram," but also "battering ram").

We began looking up the words in the Latin-English dictionary, working our way through the last four pages of *Olivia Porca*. Kimberly, who is beautiful, with two long braids that end at her waist, and a sweet and serious manner, frequently interrupted me. She was not quite as far along as Maya. "I don't want to look at her translation," Kimberly told me, "because I want to figure out all the words for myself." I loved her, too.

Soon, in the midst of thirty other kids, the three of us are in our own little Latin world, noticing which words sound like

English words, which like Spanish. When we came to the adverb *cotidie* (everyday), the two girls looked at each other, repeated the word again and again, emphasizing the "tittie" sound, and burst into peals of laughter. The only way I could get them to focus was to remind Maya that she really wanted to finish her translation that day. And she did, just before I had to leave to catch my train back upstate.

At the end of our all-too-short hour and a half, I told the girls that they should memorize one word every time we meet, and since they like *cotidie* so much, I was going to ask them to write a sentence about it next week. Stephen overheard and interjected what I would learn is one of his mantras: "And be sure to write beautiful sentences." Stephen worked hard to make everything that happens at this school embody beauty in one way or another.

I walked back to the subway in a haze of joy. *Quam mirus* Still Waters! And *quam mirus* Stephen. In his earlier career, he taught Latin and theater in Brooklyn public schools, even created a successful kids' theater group, until his beloved children turned on him, and he broke down. After retreating to his native Canada for a couple years to regroup, he decided to start his own neighborhood one-room schoolhouse. He was hoping to combat, at least for a few hours a day, the Common Core curriculum forced on the youngsters. "It's soul destroying and deadening," he believes. Although funding is always an issue, and Stephen and his family live on a shoestring, Still Waters has now been serving the community for five years and attracts first-rate poets, novelists, and nonfiction writers as volunteers.

When I arrived the following week, Kimberly rushed up to me and presented me with a folded-up piece of paper. "You can't look at it till I'm out the door," she insisted, and as she made her way to the street, where the kids were running up and down, working out their ya-yas, she kept glancing back to make sure I was waiting. Finally, she disappeared from view and I opened the paper.

Cotidie amo Anna, it said. It is the sweetest note I've ever received. (I did not have the heart to correct the nominative Anna to the accusative Annam; it seemed truly unimportant.) I loved the place, loved the kids, and loved that my Latin adventure now included helping others: true enjoyment along with benevolence. It was a very long commute, but I went every other week for the rest of the semester. As autumn turned to cold winter, the glorious warmth of learning at Still Waters in a Storm was tonic.

After the break, everyone in the class, except for Bert and me, had a new haircut. Siddhi and Alissa went one better. Alissa had become a dark, bobbed brunette, and Siddhi's hair was now short, spiky, and dyed platinum. The classroom, as usual, was overheated, and Siddhi took off his heavy, ratty sweater to reveal what looked like a brand-new tattoo on his upper arm: SPQR, the ubiquitous abbreviation for *Senatus Populusque Romanus* (the Senate and People of Rome), writ large in blue on his upper left forearm thus:

S·P·Q·R

I wondered if it was in homage to my new favorite iPhone app, SPQR, available for a mere $3.99, which features not only a Latin-to-English and English-to-Latin dictionary but also the complete works (in both Latin and English translation) of the most important Roman authors, grammar reviews, Allen and Greenough's *New Latin Grammar*, Gibbons's *Decline and Fall of the Roman Empire*, as well as entries on various aspects of Roman life. It immediately became the go-to app on my new iPhone. Whenever I was waiting and bored and hadn't brought along a book, I could read Latin poetry and translate.

It was my day to present the *Laudatio Turiae*. With over 180 lines of text engraved on two enormous marble slabs, it is the longest private inscription yet found and was likely part of Turia's enormous tomb. Because it must have cost, in the coin of the day, several million—the price of two large marbles and the cost of engraving—the one thing we know about Turia and her husband is that they were very wealthy. Other than Turia's name, their identities have been lost to time. We know they were married from references in the text, happily at least in the husband's opinion, for forty-one years. We also know that the husband supported Pompey during the Civil War, was exiled by Augustus, but later granted return to Rome.

Pieces of the stone have been found all over Rome: two of them had been repurposed as lids to *loculi*—burial urns—in the Christian catacombs and painstakingly pieced together by epigraphers. On the bottom of one fragment are the easily discerned remains of a gaming board used for *XII scripta* (a precursor of backgammon). I imagine slaves, guarding the catacombs, enjoying playing board games on the tomb lids.

Laudations for women were unusual and always private (those for men were usually held in the Forum). They became more common during Augustan Rome, when all epigraphy flourished. The *Laudatio Turiae* is unique: In all but the last two paragraphs, in which the husband decries his misery at her loss, the text directly addresses Turia as "you" as it recounts her many deeds on behalf of her (his) family. Even though Turia's parents were killed (probably during the Civil War), she managed not only to "punish the guilty" but also to maintain control of her inheritance for herself and her sister (who, because she was married, was ineligible to inherit). At that time there were two forms of marriage: *cum manu* and *sine manu*. In a *cum manu* marriage the wife was placed under the legal control of the husband. In a *sine manu* marriage the wife remained under the legal control of her father and ostensibly gained control of her property at the death of her father, though she was required to have a guardian, whether husband or male relative.

During her husband's exile, Turia also managed to send him slaves, money, and provisions. The two never had children, which the husband laments, even recounting that Turia was such a good wife she offered to divorce him so he could have children with another woman, adding that she would happily take on the role of "mother-in-law." He was outraged at the idea, though I can't help but wonder if she might have had reasons other than proving she was a good Augustan wife (Augustus held procreation to be a positive political act). Perhaps she had enjoyed her life as an independent woman while her husband was away and longed for some way to get it back.

She had been bold and brave when she was forced into the public sphere by her husband's proscription. She stood up to Lepidus, who was then consul in Rome, so vehemently that she was dragged away by the hair, like a sixties protester. I believe she must have missed her public life when her husband returned from exile and been bored when once again consigned to home life. Was she like the post–World War II women, whose taste of work and independence during the war was so brutally crushed once the men returned? I couldn't help but give my presentation a feminist spin, see it through the lens of my mother's life, this intelligent, competent woman, so limited by her husband and his family. When Bert asked why the husband went to such an expense to make the memorial, I was stumped. To prove he was the most loving husband ever? Kind of like the Donald Trump of tombstones?

Bert had an entirely different interpretation: The expense of the *Laudatio Turiae* was not undertaken by her husband to glorify his wife but to protect himself. He had been on the wrong side of the Civil War, and such a display would very publicly enshrine his current loyalty to Augustus. Since those in control still had the power of proscription, which allowed them to confiscate all of a disloyal family's possessions and kill them to boot, this was the best, most public way for Turia's husband to declare his fidelity to the emperor and keep his fortune, which evidence suggests came from her family.

Contemplating all I've learned about the *Laudatio Turiae*, and Bert's interpretation of how the seemingly selfless man, in extolling his wife's virtues, was in fact setting himself up for the future, makes me wonder if she loved him the way he claimed to love her, or if she felt enslaved by him, doing everything for him and his family, having no enterprise of her own. Maybe she was tired and took herself out.

My father had also created a dubious memorial for my mother, in the form of a red maple tree. The tree, like her name (Frances, Fritzie, Fran, et cetera), has had several incarnations. Dad had a twenty-five-foot "Red Sunset" planted on the ninth fairway of the Sequoia Country Club in Oakland, California. The kitchen window of my parents' house overlooked that fairway across the street. My mother would sit for hours at her kitchen table, playing solitaire and watching the golfers tee off and make their way down the fairway until they were obscured by the acacia trees, which grew by the fence across the street. She herself had played that fairway hundreds of times. Golf had become my parents' main activity in their later years, and my mother had been captain of the women's golf league two years in a row. That was against the rules, but I believe the other women knew that her role at the club was one of the few remaining tethers holding her against the alcoholic tide that was more and more eroding her.

The tree died a year later, after my father had moved to Alameda and stopped being a member of the club. He was hurt and outraged that they hadn't taken the time to water it rigorously after all the years and money he'd spent there. It felt to him like a travesty, a personal insult to both of them.

We planted a second Mother Memorial Red Maple at my Rhinebeck house six years later. Dad was failing fast, and for the first time since my mother's death all of us were gathered at my house. It was a beautiful September weekend, and Dad wanted to plant the tree in honor of Mom. So all of us—four kids, three spouses, and two grandchildren—dug the hole, then planted and composted and watered a ten-foot "Autumn Glory" on one side of a lichen-covered rock outcropping at the edge of my lawn. My father, terribly frail and barely able to speak, said, when we had paused after tamping the earth firmly around it, "Let's all remember Mommie."

The Autumn Glory expired the following winter, the same time my father died. It was a victim of my lawn man's overzealous weed eating, which lashed away the lower surface of the bark.

I planted a third Mother Memorial Red Maple—a fifteen-foot, very sturdy-sounding "King Crimson" tree—the year after Dad died; it seemed so important to him that Mom have a tree at my house. And, of course, the tree was also for Dad. As a matter of fact, I'm not sure, and never have been, what the connection was between Mom and a red maple. Mom wasn't an outdoor type; I don't recall her ever naming a favorite tree or flower, or doing any gardening. I think it was Dad who had always loved red maples and decided to love them in Mom's name, much the way he claimed to love their life while she drank her way out of it.

The red maple now thrives on the border between our lawn and woods. George does not like it because it is neither a native nor an ornamental tree. He would like to cut it down, but I cannot allow that. Newly bare in late October, there is a hornet's nest from last summer still clinging to its highest branch (the leader branch, George tells me, which indicates where the tree is going). Perhaps my mother wasn't content to be a tree and added the hornet's nest to make it more her own. One of her favorite expressions was "I'm so mad I could spit," and I can imagine her in perpetuity, buzzing around amidst shrubs and flowers, mad as a hornet.

The Mom Memorial Maple, like the tall stone engravings of the *Laudatio Turiae,* was the only monument made for my mother. Because she had wanted her body donated to science, there was nothing to inter, and though her name was engraved on the tombstone that my father would share with her in his hometown of Cutler, Indiana, was that for him or for her? And the tree, for him or for her? And the *Laudatio Turiae,* was that for Turia or to protect the interests and reputation of her unnamed husband?

❦

For the next class, Siddhi presented the Calendar from Antium (*Insc. Ital.* 13.2), the largest *Fasti* (calendar) unearthed so far: a wall painting 4.5 meters long and believed to date from around 60 B.C.

As usual, Bert amplified Siddhi's presentation with a disquisition on the history of the Roman calendar: The ancient agricultural calendar was lunar and included only ten months—winter was not counted (there was no agricultural activity during what would become January and February). Each year's calendar started anew at planting time in March. The empty spaces in winter obviated the need to line up solar and lunar months—that could be done at planting time. (The truth had done Ruth Nelson's statement about February being short because everybody hated it one better. In the early calendar, the Romans didn't even allow the two winter months the courtesy of a name!)

As Rome became increasingly urbanized, it was necessary for the calendar to serve political and judicial as well as agricultural needs. The lunar and solar calendars were brought into alignment, and January and February were added. Before Julius Caesar's revisions, a leap month, or *mensis intercalaris,* was added to the end of February from time to time at the discretion of the *Pontifex Maximus* (Rome's high priest).

February would be shortened to 23 or 24 days, and the intercalary month of 27 days would be added, resulting in a year with 377 or 378 days.

After Caesar's improvements, the intercalary month was dropped, and instead February would be lengthened or shortened to align the calendar with the solar year, which is why it was left short. February (*Februa, Februum,* which translates as "purification") was mostly given over to festivals for the dead and remembrance days.

As Siddhi resumed his lecture, he paced before his projected calendar, pointing out and explaining its various elements. It was a very complicated calendar. The abbreviated names of the months are arranged across the top. Because the calendar has thirteen months altogether, including the intercalary month, we know that this calendar is pre-Caesarian. There were eight days to a week, as well as a market day. The days are listed vertically beneath each month and represented by a recurring cycle of letters *A* through *H,* every ninth day being identified as a market day (*nundinae*), which was painted in red (from this we retain our expression: a "red-letter day").

There were an amazing number of festival days: My favorite was the *Violaria,* or festival of violets, in March. On that day, families privately paid homage to their dead by placing violets on their graves. It was on my birthday—violets and death, attending my birth! Obviously, Rome's climate was quite a bit warmer than ours, since usually at the time of my birthday in late March the ground is still frozen and the appearance of violets at least two months away.

Violets are profuse in my gardens and lawns in May, as they are throughout Rhinebeck. From the Gilded Age through the Depression, the violet was the world's most popular flower, the fashionable choice for corsages and nosegays (ah, nosegays, where have they gone?). And Rhinebeck was known as the Violet Capital of the World.

In those years, there were over four hundred violet greenhouses in Rhinebeck. Only one remains, though now it grows anemones, lilies, and Christmas trees. The owner, Fred Battenfeld, as a small homage to history, plants one row of cultivated violets every year—most of which go to restaurateurs for use in salads and decorations. Battenfeld's is a mile's walk from my house. Perhaps seeds from that violet farm had made the short journey by wind to my property, and I am grateful. I, too, am sometimes inspired to put them in a salad or to decorate a dessert with them.

After class, I congratulated Siddhi on his presentation, and the two of us walked to the Retreat together. At last I could ask him about the SPQR tattoo I'd been curious about all semester. The tattoo, he told me, was his second. He lifted up his T-shirt to expose his first tattoo: the biohazard symbol emblazed on his back between his shoulder blades:

"I have a double major: biology and classics," he explained, "and I wanted to have both passions represented on my body."

"Why those two symbols?" I asked.

"I love what SPQR represents, you know, the people and the Senate, even though everyone knew the emperor was pulling the strings. I love the democratic feel of it, how it stands for this huge body of people—all these populations, who had nothing in common but the empire—as one entity. I find it beautiful, like *e pluribus unum*.

"I got the biohazard sign not only because I love the way the symbol looks but I love the parts of nature that kill you. I've always admired the beauty of deadly animals—I was obsessed with dinosaurs when I was a kid, and that's what started me liking Latin, because their names were in Latin. I also love the mysteries of germs, bacteria, and viruses."

I was smitten anew. This adorable, lively young man was also formidably bright and thoughtful, not to mention sweet. I wanted to ask him if he'd like a second Mom but restrained myself.

CHAPTER 12

Festina lente.

Make haste slowly.

—Augustus

That winter was the coldest, snowiest winter we'd had in twenty years. In late November, after the first deep freeze, a flock of bluebirds appeared, accompanied by a couple of goldfinches and a few titmice. They all flew about the yard for several hours. The next day they were gone.

My resident deer family, a doe, a yearling, and a two-year-old, that usually kept to the forest or the gullies on either side of our long driveway, now slept closer to the house. They made daily forays to scavenge whatever seed the birds dropped from the feeder. Augie, at fourteen, was mostly deaf and no longer heard the approach of the deer, but he stood sentry at the French doors when he was not sleeping on the couch. When he spotted deer approaching the feeder, he'd set up a fury of barking until I let him out to chase them away. The deer would retreat to the rise just on the other side of Augie's electronic fence, taunting him as he barked and barked, *nequiquam* (in vain). Finally, I would don coat and boots and chase them away, if only to stop his incessant barking.

Familiarity bred not only contempt but also fondness, and I'd finally accepted that they live here, too. George had even named the doe Gertrude, after his grandmother. This winter, rather than longing for the city, I practiced the simple pleasures of study, both of Latin and of the wildlife on our property. It was, all and all, a Lucretian winter.

Rob Brown's Vassar course on Lucretius and Virgil began the last week of January. Attending were the same seven of us from Bert's epigraphy class, along with Alissa, who had returned to our fold. We had all become friendly in that lively class and were happy to be together for another semester. Rob seemed delighted to see us all and welcomed us in his elegant, low-key way.

"We'll begin with Lucretius then move on to Virgil. I've not taught Lucretius in a long time, but I wrote my doctoral thesis on him. Since this may be the last time I teach Virgil, I thought I'd do something I haven't tried before. We'll focus on both poets' view of the afterlife, Virgil VI and Lucretius III. Reading both, we'll see the opposite poles of ancient belief."

Lucretius has been enjoying a second renaissance in the past few years, ever since Stephen Greenblatt's 2012 best seller, *The Swerve*, which chronicles how Lucretius' masterwork, his only work, *De Rerum Natura*, was suppressed and almost lost during the Christian Middle Ages, then rediscovered during the Renaissance. Lucretius predated the antireligion writers Christopher Hitchens, Richard Dawkins, and Bill Maher (not to mention atomic physics) by two millennia: He inveighed against the superstition that the gods influence human life, and spent many verses (yes, it's an epic poem) listing all the damage done human life and society by fear of hell.

Lucretius was an Epicurean. Epicureanism in Greece and

Rome was much more complex than hedonism, with which it is often confused today. The Greek philosopher Epicurus believed pleasure was the highest good, but pleasure meant living a simple, austere life, without anxiety, without fear of death and the afterlife. The goal of life was to avoid pain, and one avoided pain by avoiding desire and attachment. Lucretius, in *De Rerum Natura,* translates the philosophy of Epicurus into Latin. Epicurus believed that the world was composed of atoms (*prima materia*) and void (*inane*), and that the soul and body, twinborn, also died at the same time: The soul could not exist without the body. Though he allowed that the gods existed, they lived in their own ethereal sphere, quite unconcerned about the doings of us mortals below.

I had no truck with the concept of gods and god. My religious upbringing was desultory. My mother had been raised Catholic and attended only Catholic schools (all that Latin!), but she left the Church when I was an infant. My brother Charles, at three, had fallen out of a two-story window onto a cement sidewalk, resulting in a six-inch skull fracture. Only the red cowboy hat he always wore held his head together. Through the long weeks in the hospital, my mother sat vigil, praying and promising god that if Charles should live, she would have a mass said for him. The priest would often remind her, "The lord giveth and the lord taketh away." It was not the consolation my mother wanted and needed. Mother identified the priest with the Church. When Charles was released from the hospital, she did have a mass said in his honor, then she left the Church. She had long disagreed with its stance on birth control, and that priest was the final straw. Had she lost her faith in god or merely the institution? She never said. Was the loss profound? She never said.

My father was a Presbyterian, but his religion seemed to be

largely prophylactic. He worried that I did not plan to baptize my daughter, Sophie. "What if you're wrong?" he asked. I'd already reasoned that if I were wrong, we'd end up in hell together with most of the other intelligent people on earth. I had considered myself an atheist since I was thirteen, when my mother, much to my alarm, enrolled me in a confirmation class at the local Lutheran church we sporadically attended. Though we weren't really Lutherans, we simply attended whatever church was closest to home. The pastor hated my questions in confirmation class and knew, I'm sure, what were my true beliefs or lack thereof. I took my First Communion and never set foot in that church again.

It wasn't until years later that I realized atheism was not a socially acceptable choice. It was during a fancy summer party in the Hamptons, populated by well-known authors, agents, and editors, that I was set straight. As was my wont in those days, before I'd learned, like my colleagues, to have interesting opinions about books I hadn't read and to comment on the current ephemeral topics popular among the chattering classes, I used to try to engage in meaningful conversation at such parties by sitting alone off to the side somewhere (as Humphrey and I had always done). I felt less anxious sitting alone than I did trying to break into conversations. Only the brave would stop to say hello, and often we would have interesting, rather than phatic, conversation. Once a powerful agent came and sat by me. I'd been contemplating some absurdity of the Moral Majority, which was the Tea Party of the eighties, when I revealed myself to be an atheist. The agent disapproved. "I really don't know why you say that. Isn't it better to say you're agnostic?"

"But I'm not agnostic," I countered. "I'm not unknowing about a supreme being. I fully believe it to be a fiction."

He spent another five minutes trying to convince me that it

would be better for me, that I'd sound friendlier and nicer, if I switched to calling myself an agnostic. "Really, what's the difference," he concluded, "and it sounds so much better."

I've always favored those who aren't afraid to speak their true minds, popular opinion be damned. The only celebrity autobiography I ever published was that of Frank Zappa, who included in his book an antireligious screed and a copy of his application to the state of Alabama to incorporate his own new religion, which he did in reaction to Alabama judge W. Brevard Hand's ruling that "Secular Humanism was, in fact, a religion and that the tenets of its faith were dominating the curriculum of Alabama's public schools, and thereby violating the civil rights of Christians."

Zappa called his church C.A.S.H., the Church of American Secular Humanism, and wrote down the Tenets of the Faith. They are still a needed corrective, all these years later:

"The people of Our Faith refuse to be persecuted any longer by a fanatical fifth column, shoveling money in the direction of 'special friends' in Washington DC."

When a higher court struck down Hand's ruling, Zappa withdrew the papers and "dissolved the religion."

Zappa once told me, "It's my job to take everything to its most absurd extreme." His was a brave and original soul if ever I've met one. He'd made his point well; Lucretius would have loved him.

Little is known about Lucretius. Some believe this to be the result of a conspiracy of silence conducted by early Christians determined to suppress the atheistic arguments made in *De Rerum Natura*. The only reference made to him was in the fourth century A.D., in the annals of St. Jerome (who is portrayed, elegantly dressed, in a portrait hanging in Vassar's

Lehman Loeb Art Center). The history records that Titus Lucretius was born in 99 B.C. He was driven mad by a love potion but managed to compose several books (which were later corrected by Cicero) between episodes of insanity. He committed suicide in 55 B.C. at the age of forty-four.

Most scholars believe none of these assertions; Lucretius' opinion of romantic love was no higher than his opinion of religion—he believed both were scourges to a peaceful life.

Rob tells us we'll go slowly at first, and the class will focus on literary analysis. He assumes we'll take care of the grammar on our own, though he assures us that we'll go through our translations line by line at the beginning. He then asks us to sight read the first ten lines, since they "aren't as difficult" as later lines. Xavier, five students away from me, offers to begin. Luckily, class ended before it was my turn. *Vah!*

A contemporary of Catullus, Lucretius set his sights on a high perch in the poetic pantheon. He wrote only in dactylic hexameter, and he consciously competed with the Greek poets (he preceded Virgil by thirty years). Lucretius is maddeningly difficult to translate: *De Rerum Natura* is didactic, it's philosophy in poetic form, and the demands of dactylic hexameter make the usual confusing placement of Latin words even more scrambled. How's that for a triple whammy?

Consequently, translating is a slow and painstaking slog. Plus, we did little translating last semester so now, after a year of not being immersed in daily translation, I've lost some of my limping mojo. It still takes me three or four hours, and two different sittings, to translate forty lines.

Lucretius begins Book III with praises of Epicurus, who laid out the void before his students:

Divina mente coorta,
diffugiunt animi terrores, moenia mundi
discedunt. totum video per inane geri res.

Because his divine mind arose,
the terrors of the soul dispersed, the walls of the world
separated. I saw everything driven through the void.

For Lucretius, a materialist, the void is not a threat but the
ground of all phenomena, through which atoms, which act as
seeds, mingle with one another to create life. At death the seeds
disperse and bounce again through the void until they coalesce
with other seeds to create a new entity. No soul remains.

This is pretty much what I've always believed: that the soul
cannot exist without the body, its container. As we continue to
translate I keep discovering—or forcing, I'm not sure which—
similarities between Lucretius and Zen Buddhism: Both believe
we are not solid, separate, or permanent. The universe is a con-
tinual unfolding, with atoms going off in different directions to
form something entirely new. Lucretius' void is not all that different from the Zen concept of emptiness. It is the ground of
being, that place of momentary silence between the busy churn-
ings of the mind, that qualityless quiet one seeks in meditation.

This sets me to stewing over the word "void." As in English,
this versatile member of the House of Ids is both noun and
adjective: *inane, inanis* (noun) and *inanis, inanis* (adjective).
The noun extends the adjective's meaning of "empty, void,
abyss" to mean also "vanity, worthlessness, an idle show." To
Lucretius, the void is simply empty reality, something with its
own form of clarity. Vanity is the rush to cover it over with
posturing, with an idle show or *persona*, which literally means
"to sound through." Thus the void "sounds through" the

persona. And what is persona but one's identity, purpose, career, ambition, all cultivated to fill otherwise empty days. Here begins the mental churn that I first experienced in college, at my first introduction to Zen Buddhism. How does one get underneath the persona? How can one exist in emptiness?

It wasn't until I was diagnosed with extremely aggressive breast cancer, with twenty-seven positive lymph nodes, and was more than likely to die within a few years, that I began to explore the Zen concepts that had been long waiting for the turn of my attention.

Though the possible death sentence failed to lead me to religion (as it had not claimed Zappa at the end, nor Hitchens), it did lead me to meditation and ultimately Zen. Fortuitously, I had begun my exploration three months before I was diagnosed with cancer. I'd read Thich Nhat Hanh's *The Miracle of Mindfulness*, and it spoke to me, spoke to slowing down, which was the thing I most needed to do. Thay (as he is known to his followers) was giving a three-day silent retreat at the Omega Institute near my home in Rhinebeck, and I signed up. I'd wanted to go the year before, but when shrink, husband, and best friend all scoffed at the idea of my being silent for three days, I opted out. The following year, determined, I went anyway. "I'm sure you'll be more silent than anyone else there," the Ablative Absolute said.

Meditation worked something of a miracle for me. It gave me something to hang on to during the months of chemo and helped me approach illness not as a battle but as an opportunity to free myself. I demoted myself from a management job back to editor. I subscribed to allopathic, homeopathic, and spiritual remedies. Though the latter were never god based: yoga, long sits meditating in the rose garden at the Cathedral Church of Saint John the Divine (now gone; in its place, a condo) and on benches along the Hudson, watching the sun set over the mighty river. My companion book was *The Tibetan Book of Living and Dying*. I also worked with a hands-on healer. Harry Bayne's method was visualization, rather than analysis; there was no god talk, only the comforting laying on of hands, and gentle questions. Once, early on, with me abed and exhausted from the effects of chemo, he asked, "Do you have any ideas about why you have cancer?"

"Drivenness," I said, the word zooming out of my mouth before I'd even thought it. "Cells moving too fast, doing their job too fast, uncontrollably driven the way I am."

"What does that look like?" he asked.

I saw myself at eight years old, at the Kiwanis Club luncheon with my father, wearing the pretty lavender dress my mother had sewn for me, my pigtails lavender beribboned. The local newspaper printed a photo of me handing my father his name tag. You can see the love in our eyes. We were alike, even then.

As the healer encouraged me to expand the image, I saw myself as a lavender-clad donkey with a stick-wielding father following close behind me. Were those the terms of his love? Or simply what I had internalized along with his love?

"What does it feel like if you stop?" the healer asked.

I couldn't visualize anything, but I could make the sound, deep in my throat, a ragged gasp of panic and fear.

"What do you see now?" he asked.

I saw the void, and I was afraid.

I still see it, and I am still afraid. Is the anxiety I scurry around to avoid in fact fear of death, as Lucretius claims? I have always thought of it as a fear of meaninglessness and purposelessness. My drivenness is antithetical to the peaceful life that Epicurus and his followers Lucretius and Horace extol. Is it part of my *prima materia* or simply my *persona*? Are my studies merely a new way of fleeing myself, of creating a new persona—Latinist—to avoid staring down the void my life might become, the void that Mother had dropped into? She had failed to create for herself a viable persona once motherhood had ended. It wasn't death she was afraid of, but life. "I'm done," she'd told me the last time I saw her. "I see no reason to stay alive except someone needs to take care of your father."

Mother died when she was only sixty-six. Our family was due to gather at home to celebrate my father's seventieth birthday, the first time we would all be together in thirteen years. Mom had been anxious about the gathering: The anticipation of making a big family dinner overwhelmed her. She had cooked and cleaned and sewed and watched as, one by one, we had moved off to college and into lives different from any she could have imagined for us. She seemed diminished by each departure, and her alcohol consumption increased.

"I think we never gave you kids enough direction," she'd complain. But what direction could she have given us, she whose only life outside the home was bridge and golf, leisure activities, not passionate pursuits? She made it clear that she'd hoped I would become someone else—who or what she couldn't say, only not who I was and definitely not someone who charted a course opposite to hers.

Only years later did I realize what Mom had wanted was intimacy in exchange for all she'd done for us: She wanted to see herself reflected in us. Yet when she looked at us she couldn't see herself at all. And when she looked at herself she saw only emptiness.

Early in the morning, seven days before we were to arrive, my mother dropped dead. I'll never know if the arrhythmia that killed her happened naturally or as the result of cigarettes, sleeping pills, and the bottle of vodka she consumed every day.

If an autopsy was ever performed, my father chose never to tell us the results.

⟡

Lucretius is a superb poet as well as a philosopher. Like Ovid, he makes his words act out his meaning.

> *Ex ineunte aevo sic corporis atque animai*
> *mutua vitalis discunt contagia motus*

> Thus, from the beginning of time, the shared union
>   of the body and soul
> learns the motions of life

The second line is what is known as a golden line: a line of dactylic hexameter, composed of only five words thus: adjective (*mutua*), adjective (*vitalis*), verb (*discunt*), noun (*contagia*), noun (*motus*). The adjectives and nouns are intertwined and visually picture the reciprocity of what is being expressed.

The term "golden line" is first attested in an obscure English grammar from 1652. It was never referred to as such by the Roman poets or rhetoricians, though they used the device extensively. Was it used to demonstrate high art or for convenience? And why is it called golden? No one seems to know.

Lucretius vividly diagnosed the drivenness that still plagued me, that had sent me running back and forth to New York for the past few years:

> If men are able, in the same way as they seem to
> perceive a weight press upon their soul and fatigue
> them with heaviness, to recognize from what things
> so great a mass of evils stand on their heart. . . .

Thus they might not live their life, as we generally see a man who does not know what he wants for himself and seeks always to change entirely as if that will enable him to put down the load. Often he goes outside . . . when he is wearied to be home, and suddenly he returns since he feels no better outside. . . . He flees himself in this way, but . . . he is not able to escape at all, therefore against his will he clings and hates . . .

Clinging and hating: This again echoes the practice of Zen meditation, which is practicing not to cling to our feelings. Lucretius describes, in many verses, what Rupert Spira, a Zen master, says in a phrase: "The two core elements of ego are a sense of lack and fear of death."

Although Lucretius allows that some suffering in life is unavoidable, he feels it is temporary and that pleasure, not suffering, is the first principle of life. Unlike Lucretius, Zen—and all Buddhist philosophy—begins with the perception that life is suffering and that the pursuit of pleasure is the root cause of most suffering.

In February, midsemester, I attended sesshin, a four-day silent retreat, with my sangha, No Traces Zendo. At the end of my year in cancerland, I had sought out a Zen teacher. I wanted to hang on to the calm I had found in chemo, and I suspected Zen, along with the Iyengar yoga I had been practicing for seven years, was the way for me. I found No Traces and Nancy Baker, a lay teacher in the Soto Zen lineage who was also a Wittgensteinian philosopher who taught at Sarah Lawrence College.

After a few years sitting and practicing with No Traces, I entered jukai—the formal rite of passage to becoming an official Buddhist. This included hand sewing a rakusu with the other students in my sangha (I was the first to finish) and copying the long Soto Zen lineage on scrolled parchment (ditto). When Nancy saw I had misspelled "Eihei Dogen" on my lineage scroll, she remarked, "Everything you do, you do fast, Jakuan. You even misspelled the name of our progenitor on your lineage because you hurried. Why are you always in such a hurry?"

Nancy gave me the dharma name Jakuan, which means Serenity, literally *Jaku-an*: peace of nirvana. She was careful to explain that a dharma name is given either to characterize your practice or to express what your practice seeks.

During sesshin, each day, after three hours of sitting, followed by breakfast, we had a ninety-minute work practice for which each of us was given a task that we were to spend the entire ninety minutes accomplishing. The tasks might include dusting bookshelves, which had been dusted the previous day during work practice; or vacuuming the floor, which had been vacuumed the previous day during work practice; or cleaning a bathroom, which had been cleaned the previous day during work practice. Not much cleaning actually needed doing.

I didn't like work practice; I found it a waste of time, even though time, during those many hours of sitting, was ever expansive. I usually tried to score a job on the third floor, which I could do quickly, then retire to my room to nap. I'd been awake since 5:00 A.M. And what was the purpose of cleaning something that didn't need cleaning?

One day I was assigned to clean Nancy's room, a 10x12-foot chamber on the second floor. I opened the door and found Nancy sitting on her bed reading. I began to dust the windowsill. "Slower, Jakuan," she said, without looking at me. I dusted more slowly. "Slower, Jakuan," she said again. I tried to go even more slowly. "Slower, Jakuan." She kept repeating "Slower, slower, slower," until finally, as I dusted, I went so slowly that I could see every crevice in the wood grain and the infinitesimal dust particles that resided there.

At some point Nancy's gaze returned to her book. I continued to dust more slowly than I'd ever dusted before. I discovered new universes of dust. One of the tables had latticework between its legs, and I folded the dust rag so that I could wedge it between the holes and slowly move it back and forth, like dental floss between teeth, to clean the base of the lattice. When the bell signaling the end of work practice rang, I hadn't entirely finished dusting the four pieces of furniture in Nancy's room.

My Latin study is another form of meditation for me, another way of slowing down, of turning off the engine. I have to translate Latin the way I cleaned Nancy's room—slowly, mindfully, meditatively—checking for embedded bits of meaning. It is impossible to work on a translation quickly. If the task I choose for this last era of my life is to learn to slow down and enjoy the moment, then Latin is my primary practice in accomplishing that.

CHAPTER 13

Haec studia adulescentiam alunt, senectutem oblectant, secundas res ornant, adversis perfugium ac solacium praebent, delectant domi, non impediunt foris, pernoctant nobiscum, peregrinantur, rusticantur.

These studies nourish youth, entertain old age, embellish success, provide refuge and solace in adversity, bring pleasure at home, do not hamper us when we are away, and are our companion through the night, on our travels, our rustication.

—Cicero

For the past two years, I had been scouring the Internet for all things Latin. I'd discovered a few "Living Latin" programs, most held during the summer. SALVI, *Septentrionale Americanum Latinitatis Vivae Institutum* (North American Institute for Living Latin Studies), offered both weeklong and weekend immersion programs at various venues around the country where Latinists lived together and spoke only Latin.

The Paideia Institute hosted summer programs in Rome and Greece, and winter-break programs in Paris, where Latin was both studied and spoken. *Paideia* is the Greek term for the humanities. *Humanitas* in Latin, these are the studies that were thought necessary to create intellectually well-rounded citizens and included grammar, geography, gymnastics, mathematics, music, natural history, and philosophy—essentially the same disciplines pictured in the Cornaro window at Vassar's Thompson Library.

I had contemplated going to a February SALVI weekend, held in an old plantation house in West Virginia, but it seemed like a long, cold, snowy trip and a bit too much of a commitment: They required attendees to sign a contract agreeing to speak only Latin during the entire weekend.

Paideia was offering a Living Latin weekend in New York, so I signed up. It seemed a lot less daunting than the idea of speaking only Latin for an entire weekend among strangers, all of whom were likely much better Latinists than I. The Paideia weekend ran from nine to five on Saturday and Sunday, with a break for lunch, and I had the refuge of a non-Latinist friend's apartment in which to revert to English Saturday evening.

One week before the event a reading packet arrived: The subject of the weekend was to be laughter, *De Risu*. The forty-page booklet included excerpts from essays by Quintilian and Cicero, a scatological satire of Claudius by Seneca the Younger, as well as antique and modern jokes (all in Latin), epigrams, riddles, nonsense poems, and dialogues. On the last page was a seventy-line poem in which every word begins with *P*, titled *"Pugna Porcorum"* ("The Fight of the Pigs"), by Publius Porcius Poeta (Poet of Pork). Why so many Latin pigs in my life?

I began reading the Cicero. My heart sank. It would take me many tens of hours to translate this; I was not ready for the weekend. I had hoped that Paideia would be my first venture into New York City's Latin community, and community was what I most longed for in this new life. I was, and would always be, an outsider as an auditor: Though my classmates and I were friendly, we would never see one another after the semesters ended, and the professors had their own world.

I decided my participation would have to wait another couple of years. I was brave but unwilling to walk into a situation where I would be entirely at sea, so I wrote Jason Pedicone, the director of the program, telling him I thought my mastery of Latin was not up to a weekend of speaking.

The next day he wrote a reassuring note, encouraging me to attend. "All levels are welcome," he wrote, "and you won't be the only novice there." And then, an hour later another e-mail arrived:

"I just checked out your Web site and now I REALLY want you to come to our conference! It's important to me to cultivate people from beyond the walls of the academy who are doing cool things like you are and who think Latin is important, as you obviously do. Last year, for instance, we had a writer from the *Boston Globe* and a documentary filmmaker show up. They were both Latin novices but had a good time, and it was great to hang out and make their acquaintances. So please come as our guest (don't pay), check out the event and our organization. I'd really like to meet you."

With me, flattery will get you everywhere: Someone REALLY wanting me? Who was I to refuse such welcome? Since it had always been my plan to follow this pursuit into whatever odd corners it led, here was a corner I was duty-bound to explore.

And perhaps it would be fun. It must be: Paideia also offered *cenae Latinae* (Latin meals) at which only Latin was spoken. Would such confabs continue if they weren't fun? I imagined it would be something like a science-fiction convention, with all the eccentric enthusiasts enjoying one another's company.

Over the past two years, I'd become more and more aware of the similarities between classicists and science-fiction enthusiasts; in truth, classicists seemed like a kind of subset of the science-fiction world. I knew Siddhi was into science fiction. He wore an orange bracelet inscribed with "Follow the creed. Live by the creed." When I asked him what that stood for (as any good epigrapher would), he explained it was from *Assassin's Creed*, a science-fiction game he played online. I knew Alissa was a fervent science-fiction fan, too, as was Ben Stevens.

As David Hartwell, the top science-fiction editor of my era, once explained, "The reason for all the conventions is because science fiction attracts people who don't fit in anywhere, so they like to imagine their own worlds. They can choose their own reality and find others equally passionate about it, and the only requirement for entry is enthusiasm." Wasn't that a fairly accurate description of Latinists?

Emboldened by Jason's welcome, I contacted Stephen Haff at Still Waters in a Storm. I'd told him about the Living Latin weekend, which he would have very much liked to attend but he couldn't afford the fee. I decided that if Jason wanted me to come for free, he would want Stephen even more, so I put the two together via e-mail.

Three days before the seminar, I received an e-mail from Curtis, who had seen my name on the list of attendees. He would be teaching there. What luck! I would know someone!

Two days before the seminar, the snow began upstate, heavy and relentless. It continued all day and all night. By the time the storm abated, thirty-six hours later, it had dropped three feet of snow. For the next day George and I, housebound, listened hopefully for the sound of the snowplow coming up our long driveway. It did not come. I was supposed to be in New York City already, but there was no way I could even get down the driveway. George had ventured out a few times on his snowshoes, first to clear a path for Augie, who, after looking warily at the wall of snow he had to step into, finally did, only to sink like a stone. George had to shovel in three layers, a foot at a time. We surmised the plows had to do the same, which was why they were taking so long.

Stephen had e-mailed saying he was planning to meet me at the conference with four of the kids. Snow doesn't stop the city for more than a few hours. Up here it can stop us for days. Finally, at 2:00 A.M. Saturday, the snowplows arrived. It took two hours, thrice as long as usual, for them to plow from our garage to the road. Finally the path was clear, and I caught the 7:00 A.M. train into the city.

I always take a seat on the west side of the train, so I can watch the river. That morning the Hudson was completely blanketed by snow; even the line of the shipping channel, a narrow ribbon for navigation kept open by an icebreaker, was clogged by snow-covered ice floes. Just below Poughkeepsie, I spotted a trio of coyotes walking single file on the frozen river from shore to island. Half an hour later, by the time we'd passed Croton-on-Hudson, the river was water again, glinting through jagged sheets of ice atop which raptors sat. I spotted three bald eagles, patron bird of George. Just before reaching Manhattan, the Hudson was flowing freely, teeming with barges rather than birds.

I disembarked and tromped through the already dirty, slushy snow to the Lincoln Center Campus of Fordham University, where the conference was being held. I arrived just at nine, and the place was already abuzz with activity: The attendees were recognizably classicists, most of them thin, young men. I later spotted two other elders; both turned out to be newly retired lawyers who had been Latin majors in college and were now working toward teacher certification. Everyone there, sixty in all, was either a graduate student or a teacher. I was the only exception. Now I understood why Jason so wanted me to come.

I heard the mostly incomprehensible hum of Latin being spoken all around me, which sounded a lot like Italian. Jason Pedicone recognized me and came up to introduce himself. A tall, thin, thirtysomething man with a Gladwellian nimbus (Latin *nimbus,* cloud) of strawberry-blond hair, he welcomed me in English and assured me that the seminars were tracked by level and I would be fine. He was quickly whisked away by a Latin speaker, and I found a place among those seated awaiting the beginning of the session.

One latecomer made a remarkable entrance: He was wearing a bristling bearskin coat, large galumphing boots, and looked like Davy Crockett. As he slowly shed layer after layer of outer garment, many of the participants gathered around him, greeting him in Latin. Finally he emerged, another tall, skinny man in his thirties. He looked like a grown-up Siddhi and exuded the same sexy aura, though his style was more mountain man than Goth.

Soon Jason stepped up to the podium and welcomed us first in Latin, then in English. He began with a poem by Yeats, which was projected on the screen behind him:

The Scholars

Bald heads forgetful of their sins,
Old, learned, respectable bald heads
Edit and annotate the lines

That young men, tossing on their beds,
Rhymed out in love's despair
To flatter beauty's ignorant ear.

All shuffle there; all cough in ink;
All wear the carpet with their shoes;
All think what other people think;
All know the man their neighbour knows.
Lord, what would they say
Did their Catullus walk that way?

"Here we prefer to walk like Catullus," he assured us, as he smoothed his receding hairline, "even if we're going bald."

Most of the heavies of the Living Latin movement were in attendance. Terence Tunberg and Milena Minkova ran the classics program at the University of Kentucky, the only university program in America that conducted classes in Latin. They also hosted a summer, weeklong Latin immersion program. Nancy Llewellyn, the founder of SALVI, was also there. All three gave lectures in Latin, very little of which I could understand.

There was also a lecture in English, by Anna Andresian, a diminutive whirlwind of energy who had taught both at SALVI and the University of Kentucky program. She had developed a sign language to help students understand the declensions. "I'm going to stand on this table so you all can see me," she said, and then began to demonstrate her semaphores, which were brilliant, and included not only the declensions but also all the verb moods and tenses, including subjunctive and deponent. She explained some of the logic behind the semaphores: The nominative was the left hand held up, fingers spayed to introduce the sentence. The genitive was the right hand tapping the wrist, to connote ownership. My favorite was the dative, where the right hand opened and closed toward the left "shooting sparks of influence," as she explained. This expressed the dative not only as an indirect object meaning "to" or "for" but also as something that was indirectly influenced by the verb in other ways, such as the dative of possession, the dative of reference, and her favorite, the dative of reference with genetic force. She gave the example of the latter, in sign language, of *canis manum mihi mordet* (the dog bites my hand). The dative *mihi* rather than the possessive adjective *meam* is used here to emphasize the impact of the bite, rather than the ownership of the hand.

Each day we also had four classroom sessions. My first, much to my delight, was with Curtis. He started by asking each of the ten of us to introduce ourselves: *Nomen mihi Anna est, habito Rhinebeck.* We discussed humor and came up with adjectives to describe it, most of which had been in the Catullan lexicon: *urbanitas, venustus, salsus, facetus, iocus, dicacitas.* Curtis was very good at acting out words we didn't know, reminding me how much I missed him, his passion and excitement for Latin, his sense of play, and his adorable nerdiness.

Though I could understand much of what was being said in Latin, when it came my turn to speak, my mind went blank or reverted to French. When I mentioned this problem to Nancy Llewellyn, she assured me that I was encountering what she called linguistic interference, and that the brain would adjust to a new language after three days of solid exposure.

By the end of the weekend, I'd memorized the most common words the various teachers used in conversation: *Fortasse* (perhaps) and *igitur* (therefore) function much as we have come to use "like," as a connective pause. *Ita* was used for yes and *minime* for no—whether those were what the Romans used, no one could say for certain, but this group had adopted them as such.

Terence Tunberg knew dozens of surprising words in Latin. "The Romans had more words for everyday stuff than you will ever learn if you only read poetry," he told us. Among them were *propoma* (cocktail) and *cervisia* (beer). He himself had coined a word for high heels, *calceaenta fulta*. The next morning I could tell that those three things had been much in evidence at the dinner I didn't attend the night before. I overheard Mountain Man Hottie saying to someone, "I didn't get in till three!" There might even have been sex, drugs, and rock 'n' roll!

Mountain Man Hottie, in the seminar I had with him, was incandescently brilliant and witty, even in Latin. I spoke with him afterward, because in the introductions that began each session, I learned that he lived in the Catskills and had been making maple syrup. "My fellow is a maple syrup maker," I told him. "We live in Rhinebeck, where are you?" I was hoping to strike up a friendship with this adorable man, thinking that, as with Siddhi, if you're too old to try to seduce them, why not adopt them? John Byron Kuhner (Byron!) lived about fifty miles west of us in the middle of the Catskills, but that's all I learned before a beautiful blonde interrupted and he was lost to me.

Near the end of the last day, Stephen Haff arrived with four of the Still Waters kids: my beloved Kimberly, along with three others, Leo, Stella, and Olivia. We spent twenty minutes in the hall outside the classroom, speed-translating the first of the *Nugae Iocosae* (Funny Trifles) that would be our text for the hour. It was a riddle:

> *Ego sum principium mundi*
> *Et finis saeculorum.*
> *Per me omnia continentur,*

Sine me nihil est.
Sum trinus et unus
At tamen non sum deus.

I am the principle of the world
And the end of the ages.
Everything is contained through me,
Without me nothing exists,
I am three and one
But, nevertheless, I am not a god.

None of us could come up with the answer before class began. Curtis, by happy chance, was the leader of the seminar and warmly welcomed our "young students from Still Waters." He began by asking if one of them wanted to read the riddle in Latin. I nudged Kimberly; she read the Latin flawlessly.

She was rewarded with applause, turned to me and whispered, "That's the first time I've ever read out loud without being shy."

The class quickly came up with the answer to the riddle: time. While all of this took place in Latin, Stephen quietly translated to the two kids on either side of him, and I to those on either side of me. Then Stephen raised his hand. "Olivia has come up with a different answer," he said. "Is it okay if she says it in English?"

Olivia smiled and said. "Life."

Clearly Latin was not dead here. And indeed not even in the riddle. Because the original answer, I later learned, is the letter *m*, which comes at the beginning of *mundi* (world) and the end of *saeculorum* (ages), and its shape is three in one.

The weekend turned out to be propitious in many ways. Stephen and Jason had a long meeting after the conference and within a few weeks had set up a formal partnership that institutionalized Latin study at Still Waters. They named the program *Aequora,* which means "an even surface" or "the sea in its calm, smooth state." From then on, Stephen and I would be joined by some of the Living Latin attendees, as well as students from a high school associated with Paideia, to tutor the kids in Latin. I had found a new community, as interesting and varied as my lost publishing community. The only problem was, it, too, was in New York City. Would the city never let me go?

Back at Vassar on Tuesday morning, tromping through the snow, I ran into Bert Lott.

"I went to the Living Latin weekend in New York last weekend," I told him. "It was amazing, and Curtis was there, too."

"Ah," he said with a wry smile, "the Civil War reenactors of classical studies."

Within the small community of philologists and Latinists, there are two camps: those who favor Living Latin, approaching and teaching the language as one would a modern language; and the traditionalists, who want to retain the language as a purely written, dead language, which there is no reason to speak. Even traditionalists allow that reading aloud is essential when learning poetry, because the meter enhances meaning. They draw the line, however, at trying to fit Latin into modern speech.

"There's no use learning how to order coffee in Latin," they argue, "as there's nowhere to do such a thing except at some event made up simply to facilitate such useless endeavors."

Others believe that speaking makes learning the language more fun and engaging, not to mention that adding verbal, aural, and kinesthetic exercises to language acquisition complements the purely visual learning of the traditional method and liberates Latin from a purely heady domain by introducing a social sphere. Some, and I suspected that Bert is one of them, make fun of the Living Latinists.

I, however, was all for them. Jason asked me to be on the advisory board of Paideia, which I happily agreed to do. I was so thrilled with the idea of having a new community that I assured him I was available for anything he wanted me to do. "Would you be willing to read a friend's manuscript?" he asked me. "He was at the weekend, and you may have had a class with him: John Byron Kuhner, he has a Web site you can look at." Byron! Mountain Man Hottie! Of course I'd be delighted to read his manuscript!

I looked at John Byron Kuhner's Web site: a blizzard of entries on a vast range of topics. As well as a Latinist, he was a latter-day Thoreau who, for the past six years, had been living in a one-room cabin without running water and only sporadic electricity. He wrote about this, that, and everything, from the erudite to the trivial, on his Web site. He was a scholar and philosopher by nature as well as a naturalist and involved with many Catskill organizations.

I showed George his Web site. He took one look and said, "That's the guy I told you about, remember, the Latinist?" I remembered he had mentioned a Latinist, a fellow follower of Michael Kudish, although I had paid little notice. I now did. What were the chances of George and me independently meeting someone who embodied both our eccentric interests? I called that a cosmic connection and the sort of coincidence that made me feel I was doing what I was supposed to be doing in life.

I read John Byron Kuhner's manuscript, which was more a philosophical exploration of Christianity, Islam, and atheism than a novel, then invited him to dinner. He was fascinating.

His father had been a Catholic priest, who left the priesthood when his mother was eight months pregnant. The two never married, though they had two more children. John Byron had taught Latin in New Jersey schools for years, until his father's death and the dissolution of his marriage, after which he followed Thoreau's example and "went to the woods because I wished to live deliberately, to confront only the essential facts of life, and see if I could not learn what it had to teach, and not, when I came to die, discover that I had not lived."

What a treat it was to get to know such a character. He was one of the deepest, most sophisticated thinkers I'd ever met. He seemed somehow to have combined Lucretian and Buddhist ideas with Christianity to find something very similar to the principles on which Stephen Haff founded Still Waters in a Storm, a radical and reliable form of acceptance and love.

CHAPTER 14

Time present and time past
Are both perhaps present in time future,
And time future contained in time past.

—T. S. Eliot, "Burnt Norton"

Harbingers of spring, in the form of bluebirds and robins, arrived just as the second half of Rob Brown's class began. We would be reading and translating Book VI of *The Aeneid*, Aeneas' trip to the underworld. As it was now officially spring, Persephone would be making her way up from the underworld into the sunny realms of her mother, Demeter. Perhaps we would pass her on our way down below.

Rob introduced Virgil by telling us that it was because of Virgil that he had decided to become a Latinist. He'd started taking Latin at age eleven, but it was when he was sixteen, and read Virgil's first Eclogue, that he found his future path. "I was from a rural area of England, and those first lines sent a ringing bell of recognition in me."

That night I looked up the lines:

Tityre, tu patulae recubans sub tegmine fagi
silvestrem tenui Musam meditaris avena;

nos patriae finis et dulcia linquimus arva.
Nos patriam fugimus.

You, Tityrus, lying under the canopy of a spreading
    beech
considering the woodland Muse on slender reed;
we are leaving our country's boundaries and sweet
    fields.
We have fled our country.

Rob couldn't have known, at the tender age of sixteen when he first read those lines, that he, too, would flee his patria and become an exile. But perhaps, as Virgil would so eloquently demonstrate, the future is always present in the past.

I was happy to finally be reading Virgil, the undisputed grand master of Latin poetry. I had prepared for class by reading a new translation of *The Aeneid* by Robert Fagles during our two-week break, and was pleasantly surprised to discover that it was a true page-turner. I hadn't read the epic poem since college. In the one classics class I took while at Berkeley, we had, in three short months, plowed through *The Iliad, The Odyssey, The Persian Wars, The Peloponnesian Wars,* and Sophocles' *Theban Plays* (in English, of course). Only at the end of the quarter did we turn to the Romans, reading a bit of Ovid, Propertius, and finishing up with *The Aeneid.*

I hadn't loved *The Aeneid* anywhere near as much as I loved *The Odyssey,* which became my metaphor for my own progress in the publishing world.

What a difference age makes in the way we read! As a youth I had found Aeneas a neurotic hero compared to Achilles and Odysseus. Now I identified with all the complexities he had to endure, the troubles that fate forced on him, the tensions between love and duty, past and future, his displacement and long voyage in search of a new homeland. There is a kind of sadness to Aeneas, even in the midst of triumph. Though lacking a heroic destiny, my journey over the past few years had not been unlike that of Aeneas: perpetually poised between past and future, mourning and hope. And I was learning, as he did, that acceptance, perhaps even serenity, might be found not by forgetting the past but by remembering and honoring it. This, I realized, was one of the many things my Latin studies were doing for me. They were reconciling me with my long-dead mother. When I embarked on this Latin journey, I was running away from her legacy; but instead, I had run right into her. I was doing something she would have wished me to do, something she herself had loved.

⁂

The future is present all over Book VI of *The Aeneid:* Aeneas lands at Cumae to seek out the Sybil who will lead him to the underworld, but the city of Cumae, just west of modern Naples, was not founded until the seventh century B.C., long after Aeneas. In the underworld, Aeneas' father, Anchises, shows him the future heroes of a Rome that does not yet exist.

Virgil writes most of his epic in the historical present tense, which not only lends it immediacy but also melds past and present throughout the narrative; the past is sitting shotgun with the present as they move in tandem into the future. As Fagles writes in his afterword, "In the light of the historical present, hindsight may make a bit more sense as foresight than we thought."

As we progressed through Book VI, the mastery of Virgil's poetry was unmistakable. This passage describes his and the Sibyl's entry into the underworld:

Ibant obscuri sola sub nocte per umbram
perque domos Ditis vacuas et inania regna.

Dark, they went through the shade under the lonely
    night
and through the vacant houses and empty kingdom
    of Dis.

No English translation can capture the ghostly mood of
sola sub nocte per umbram, nor Virgil's brilliant use of hyp-
allage, one of the hallmarks of his style: One would expect
obscurus (dark) to modify *nox* (night), and *solus* (lonely) to
modify the subjects (they), but Virgil switches the relations for
poetic effect.

And here again, in the second line is Lucretius' *inania,* the
void. But Virgil's underworld is not void for long: As he and
the Sibyl approach the gorge of hell, they meet bad conscience,
disease, bleak old age, dread, hunger, poverty, and war in the
vestibule. There, too, is the huge, ancient tree where false
dreams cling to each leaf. Dis's realm hosts every monster
known to man, as well as the shades of children, suicides, con-
demned men, and those who perished of love, eternally wan-
dering the Fields of Mourning. Stranded on Lethe's banks for
one hundred years are shades of the unburied.

In Latin, *Dis* is synonymous with Pluto, god of the underworld, but the word *dis* is also a form of the adjective *dives,*
meaning "wealth." What might that mean to a Roman? Perhaps it's the wealth of the Elysian Fields, the lovely part of the
underworld, where Aeneas meets his father Anchises and learns
his fate. I enjoy anew the irony of that name, which graced the
street where I grew up.

Over the course of our translating, I even managed to

shoehorn two Buddhist concepts into Virgil's depiction of hell, the two Lucretius left out of his own philosophy: Life is suffering (as we see Aeneas, suffering the weight of his own future) and souls are reincarnated. At one point in the journey, Anchises explains that the spirits gathered at the River Lethe are those who, after being punished for their earthly sins, now drink the water of forgetfulness before they return for another life on Earth. Virgil is alone among the classic Roman writers in positing rebirth, or reincarnation (though he never calls it that—the word comes from the Latin for flesh [*caro, carnis*] and literally means "to become flesh again").

In May, along with Aeneas and the Sibyl, we left the underworld:

> *Sunt geminae Somni portae, quarum altera fertur*
> *cornea, qua veris facilis datur exitus umbris;*
> *altera candenti perfecta nitens elephanto*
> *sed falsa ad caelum mittunt insomnia manes.*
> *His ubi tum natum Anchises unaque Sibyllam*
> *prosequitur dictis portaque emittit eburna*

> There are twin doors of sleep, one which is said to be
>   made of horn,
> which gives easy exit to true shades
> the other shining with brilliant ivory,
> but through it the shades send false dreams to the sky.
> Having said these words, Anchises escorts his son
>   and the Sibyl
> and sends them both out through the ivory door.

And here again is my old friend *insomnia: sed falsa ad caelum mittunt insomnia manes* (but through it the shades send false dreams to the sky). The word clearly means "dreams," not sleeplessness, though scholars have been perplexed for centuries about why Aeneas left the underworld through the Gate of Ivory, the gate of false dreams, since everything Anchises told him came true, at least for a few centuries. Could Virgil have suspected, even then, that the empire would finally collapse and disappear?

Some commentators posit that because Aeneas and the Sibyl weren't dead, they could not exit through the Gate of Horn, the gate of true dreams. Some believe it presages the fact that Aeneas does not remember his experiences in the underworld just as he does not recognize the future emblazoned on the shield Venus has forged for him in Book XI. Others would eliminate the line altogether.

Virgil frequently uses the word *somnia* for dreams. As in English, in Latin *in* as a prefix can mean "not" but also "inside or into," so *insomnia* can be translated literally as "not sleeping" and *insomnium* as "inside sleeping" or what we experience in sleep. The word "insomnia" brings not only dreams but also nightmares and wakefulness. I am not alone in being flummoxed by this word, and it's that versatile *in*'s fault.

Robert A. Kaster in *Guardians of Language* calls the word, and the ambiguity between the feminine singular *insomnia* (sleeplessness) and the neuter plural *insomnia* (dreams or nightmares, Latin makes no distinction between them), "a minor bog of Latin lexicography."

Such bogs (*paludes*) abound when a language contains so much ambiguity, all the true authorities are dead, and the copied versions that have come down to us frequently differ. This fact gives rise to the oft-repeated Latinist phrase *lectio difficilior potior* (the more difficult reading is better), which means that when different manuscripts contain different words, the one whose meaning is less obvious is preferred.

This principle was stated first by Erasmus in the fifteenth century, when he discovered that copyists tended to simplify difficult texts. Since nearly all Latin literature comes to us in copies, made mostly by monks or professional copyists who were not as dexterous with the subtleties of language as the original authors, many commentators follow the dictum. So if two manuscripts render the same section differently, and both variants are grammatically plausible and make logical story sense, the more difficult variant is deemed better. It is this principle that sometimes sends our class down the back alleys and obscure byways of the ablative and dative cases.

It also turns on its head the scientific principle known as Occam's razor, or *lex parsimoniae* (the law of parsimony) in its original Latin. The *American Heritage Dictionary* defines it thus: "A rule in science and philosophy . . . interpreted to mean that the simplest of two or three competing theories is preferable."

The principle was devised two centuries before Erasmus by William of Ockham, an English Franciscan friar, scholastic philosopher, and theologian. Here philosophy and philology part ways. And which is more complicated? Philology, of course, at least when it comes to Latin study. *Ohe!* (Enough!)

I found myself stepping into many bogs while marveling at the visual immediacy and imaginative beauty of Virgil's underworld that semester. It was beginning to feel like the more I knew, the less I knew. It was yet another sticky relationship among past, present, and future.

Perhaps the great Virgil is correct, and the seeds of our future are contained in the distant past. The future waits for the unknowing past and present to catch up to it. My own future took twenty years to catch up to me. Among the furniture and books I had taken from my grandparents' house were two prints I had found in the music room. The two pictures had remained rolled up in a cardboard tube for twenty years. I framed and hung them only after I'd finished rebuilding my house. One was a portrait of a curly-haired blonde girl playing with her cat. The girl looked a lot like Sophie, who loves cats. Though I was allergic, she had two at her father's house, and they were her best playmates.

The other print was a kitschy primitive-realistic painting of a house surrounded by flowers, a man leaning on a shovel, smiling at a woman tending her roses, while another woman hangs a birdcage from the wisteria-garlanded front porch. The house pictured was almost identical to mine: An eyebrow colonial with the same three eyebrow windows on the second floor, the same four larger-paned windows on the first. Even the flowers were the same as those that had been planted before I'd moved in: two cultivars of old-fashioned peonies, bright pink and pale pink and white, yellow-brown irises, and a small tree in the same position on the lawn. Pliny, I learned, wrote that peonies were protected by woodpeckers and might be used for prophetic dreams, though he doesn't say how. Could it be that the peonies in that picture, and in my garden, and the woodpeckers that visit us were avatars from the future, long waiting for me?

Was there something I recognized in this house the first time I saw it that rang an unconscious bell with that picture? I once had a session with my friend Susan, a "seer" who channels the African spirit Garuda. Garuda claimed that I was being watched over by a tall, thin, white-haired man. "Did I recognize him?" she asked. "Of course," I said, "it must be my grandfather, the only other literary person in our very small clan."

When my English friend Caroline saw the newly framed print, she said, "I always thought when you were with the man in that picture, you'd finally be happy." On her next visit, two years later, she added, "And now you are. Doesn't he look like George?"

The man in the picture has the same sort of sharp nose and tanned face, hair the same color as George's, and he wears similar layers: work shirt over long-sleeved undershirt, pants too big for him, Amish-style hat. Though he isn't as skinny as George, he has the same sweet, loving expression as he looks at his wife that I enjoy when George looks at me.

Had my grandfather, like Anchises, seen my future?

CHAPTER 15

Salva res est, saltat senex.

The thing is saved, the old guy is still dancing.

—Unknown (preserved by Servius)

At semester's end, I had the equivalent of an under-graduate Latin major. I was given an unexpected graduation present. Jason Pedicone invited me to join Paideia's "Living Latin in Rome" program for a couple of weeks if I wanted. And how I wanted to study and speak Latin in its home! With Jason's help, and the first two chapters of this book, I applied for an apartment at the American Academy of Rome, and I was accepted as a visiting scholar. Six weeks later, I found myself in the multilayered glory that is Rome, where the past is ever present.

I was fortunate enough to be assigned a one-bedroom apart-ment on the top floor of the Greenhouse at the Villa Aurelia, a short hop above the Academy, on the crest of the Janiculum, the highest hill in Rome. Luigi, a friendly Italian, led me up the cobblestone drive, bordered by tufa walls, down which abun-dant blue and white flowers cascaded. I'd entered another world, of grace, gardens, and wealth. In the distance I spotted the magnificent beaux arts Villa Aurelia, glowing gold in the midmorning July sun. We turned right before the villa and headed up the narrow stone staircase, awash with flowers, to the Greenhouse, a stone structure with a tiled patio. As Luigi showed me around the charming, light-filled apartment that would be mine for two weeks, exhilaration quickly overcame jet lag. I decided to go to that afternoon's class, which was a long, lovely walk along the Tiber to St. John's University Rome Campus in the Prati neighborhood, where Paideia held its classes.

This was the fifth year of Paideia Institute's Living Latin in Rome program. The program was heir to a legendary Latin summer class given in Rome by a wildly eccentric Carmelite monk named Reginald Foster (Reginaldus to his students). A native of working-class Milwaukee, Father Foster had served as secretary to three different popes and as senior Latinist to John Paul II. In addition to translating the Vatican's public proclamations into Latin, Father Foster was a one-man Latinist band. One of his official duties was to teach Latin at the Pontifical Gregorian University, and he allowed anyone interested to join his class free of charge. He quickly became something of a cult figure, and his classes grew and grew, to the chagrin of the Vatican.

Often unbathed and unkempt, clad always in a blue polyester jumpsuit bought annually from JC Penney, he was known as the best Latinist alive. Because he came of age pre-Vatican II, when Latin was still the language of the Church, he was as close as any modern could come to a native Latin speaker. He was also a showman, a formidable teacher, and a passionate taskmaster. When exasperated to the point of indignation at the failings of some student, he would let loose a lion's roar of outrage. "If you don't know why that's subjunctive, why don't you go ask the driver of the 64 bus!" he'd yell. "Every bum and prostitute in the city spoke Latin fluently, so you can, too." He did not use textbooks but threw students from day one into Latin texts, and supplemented them with exercises he composed himself. On Sundays, Father Foster took his classes on optional excursions around Rome to read texts in the places they had been composed for: Cicero's *Catilinarian Orations* in the Forum, Augustus' *Res Gestae* at the Ara Pacis.

Jason had taken Father Foster's summer course in 2004 and liked it so much that he spent the entire next year taking every class Reginald offered and reading as many Latin texts as he could in the Biblioteca Nazionale in his spare time.

"Reginald was a genius," Jason told me. "He was a rock star, a charismatic. He could hold a room spellbound for six hours a day, six days a week. And he did that for more than twenty years!"

In 2008, halfway into the summer program, Father Foster fell seriously ill, too ill to continue the course. Jason and his friend Leah Whittington stepped in: Both were attending the class, and working on PhDs at Princeton. The two of them took over and did their best to channel Father Foster's energy and teaching methods.

At the end of the summer, Jason returned to Princeton to work on his doctoral dissertation. "I was a miserable academic," he said. "I was not well suited for long hours of study in libraries. I was an organizer, I wanted to be out and about making things happen. And I'd spent all this time getting my PhD. What was I to do with it?"

Two years later, doctorate in hand and despair in heart, he fled to Paris to regroup. At the École Normale Supérieure, as a *pensionnaire étranger,* he organized an unofficial course called *Vergilius Vivus,* in which students read and discussed *The Aeneid* in Latin. Then he got a call from Eric Hewett, a talented linguist who was also an alumnus of Father Foster's summer programs. Eric had been traveling around Europe for the past eight years, learning languages, taking on odd jobs here and there to supplement a small inheritance from his grandmother. He was living in a van at the Circus Maximus in Rome. "Hey Jason, we need to start a summer program, take over from Reggie before someone else does." And thus began Paideia. The two called Father Foster, seeking his blessing, which they duly received.

It turned out that Jason and Eric were born entrepreneurs; if Father Foster was a Latin missionary, Jason was a visionary and Eric a Latin CEO. After two years, they had attracted a solid complement of donors and students; after four, Paideia was well on its way to becoming the "go-to" organization for classical summer travel.

In this fifth Paideia summer, there were forty students divided into three groups: *juniores* (beginners), *peritiores* (skilled), and *seniores* (advanced), each taught by a Reginaldian.

Jason put me in the *juniores* group, the easiest. I tried not to feel bad about it. My classmates were in their early twenties, from Ivy League schools, save a few known as "the British invasion," clearly upper-class kids, one of whom, I could tell by the tilt of his head, was already well on his way to becoming a dandy. The British girls seemed to be taking turns on his arm, day by day. To my delight, there was also a fellow *senex*, Daniel.

The classes were much like those at Vassar and included reading, translation, and explication of the grammar of Latin texts Jason had gathered, which corresponded to the ancient sites we would be visiting.

That first day, the subjunctive and the sequence of tenses, things I'd avoided pummeling into my brain, were explained, explained again, then practiced *sub arboribus* (under the trees), which took place after a gelato break. We gathered in the school's graceful courtyard, complete, of course, with fountain, where we broke up into even smaller groups and did round-robin exercises in speaking Latin.

I hadn't improved a bit since February. Getting even a few words out of my mouth in the proper sequence with the right conjugations and tenses was nigh impossible. I blamed jet lag and the fact that the rest of the class had already been there practicing for three weeks, but I knew the real culprit: age. Daniel suffered as much as I, though he didn't seem to mind being bettered by youths who had taken a mere year or two of Latin. *Vae mihi!* (Woe is me!)

Daniel was staying near the Campo de' Fiori, so we cabbed there and dined together. Daniel had been in class since the beginning of the program, and his feet had given out. He took cabs to and from class, and thrifty me was only too happy to hitch a ride with him, share dinner, then walk the steep mile uphill to my Janiculum home, thus working off the pasta and bread I could not resist gorging on.

A working-class boy, Daniel had dropped out of school at age fourteen to work as a teller at a bank in an Italian neighborhood in Melbourne, Australia. There, one of his regular customers noticed his fluency in Italian, which Daniel had easily picked up on the job. The man convinced him to return to school and arranged a scholarship to university.

"I always loved difficult languages," Daniel told me, "so I majored in Chinese and Russian. I finished in 1968, just when diplomatic relations were being reestablished with China, and, as you might imagine, there weren't many Aussies who spoke Chinese so I become a diplomat." After eight years in China he went back for his doctorate and then divided his life between diplomatic duties and teaching Chinese at Sydney University. He was now retired, widowed, and had a brain, like mine, that needed feeding.

Back at the manse, I fell into sleep immediately.

I was awakened at dawn, this time by the sweet singing of birds, two answering each other in the longest, most musical birdsong I'd ever heard, and in the background, a call that sounded like human laughter (which George would later recognize as a laughing gull). After that melodious awakening, I easily fell back to sleep and didn't awaken again until noon, thus missing Paideia's visit to the Aventine Hill and the Knights of Malta Priory.

I walked down to the splendid Academy building for lunch, a copious vegetarian buffet prepared by graduates of Alice Waters' Sustainable Food Project. The lunch line formed against the back wall of the courtyard, which featured inscriptions, most broken and partial, a few complete, plastered into the wall. As I waited, I tried to decipher:

D M
AELIA.MARINA
SEBIBA.FECIT.AURELIO.
BASSO.CONUIGI.B.M.
ET.FILIS SUIS
LIBERTIS.LIBERTABUS
QUE.POSTERIS
QUE.EORUM

I was troubled not only by *Sebiba*, which didn't seem like a name, but also by the *libertabus*, which would be dative or ablative plural, but what did that mean? From Bert Lott's class, only six months ago, I knew a freed slave was *libertus, liberti,* a second-declension noun back-formed from the adjective *liber.* A freed female slave was *liberta, libertae,* a first-declension noun—so where did the third-declension inflection *-abus* come from?

And wasn't it unusual for a woman to have created a memorial? I needed a Latinist much better than I to sort out this one.

The woman in line behind me noticed my study and asked, "Are you a classicist?"

"I've been studying, auditing classes, for the past four years, and writing a book about it," I told her. "And you?"

"Yes, I'm a classicist here studying," she said tersely. She was a Miss Grundy type, my age, I suspect, but with the stereotypical dowdy aspect of a true scholar. She had probably already clocked me as a dilettante. Before I asked for her help, I figured I'd better embellish my credentials. I said, "I'm here with Paideia Institute. Have you heard of them?"

"Oh yes," she said, mouth in a grimace.

"Did you ever take a class with Reginald Foster?"

"Oh, no," voice dismissive, "he's not universally admired. Many think his method too much disregarded the literature."

That surprised me. I had heard nothing but the greatest praise of Reginald Foster, but here was an old-style academic who probably believed the point of language acquisition was to facilitate literary analysis.

A few days later, while touring the library, I saw her ensconced in a carrel down in the bowels of the building, where the raw materials of researchers lived. Books were piled like a fortress around her computer. She was the sort of scholar Jason did not want to be, and she was holding firm against the Reginaldian approach he had embraced.

I had to wait until I returned from Rome and could seek Curtis' and Bert's help to sort out the inscription, which, properly translated, was:

To the Gods of the Shades
Aelia Marina

while she was still alive made this
for Aurelius Bassus
her most deserving husband
and for their children
and for their freedmen and freedwomen
and for their descendants.

It turned out *Sebiba* was an error in inscription, which should have read *se viva* (herself living)—a common formula for making a tomb for yourself. The *libertabus* was also standard for inscriptions, the *abus* added in the dative and ablative plural to distinguish the feminine form from the masculine, freedwomen from freedmen. Not unlike the backwards *C*.

Errors in insciption were, of course, common and usually uncorrectable. Marble was expensive, even then, as was the fee for the inscriber, some of whom were a lot better than others.

This also explains the widespread use of abbreviations in inscriptions, a necessary money-saving shortcut, just as the compactness of the Latin language may be explained by the writing materials available at the time. Most common were wooden tablets covered with wax. A stylus, sharpened on one end for writing, flattened on the other for smoothing mistakes, inscribed the letters in the wax, and the entire tablet could be remelted and then reused.

I suspect there would be much less *insanabile cacoethes scribendi* in our own time were writing materials so expensive and the act of writing itself so time-consuming.

I had been to Rome only once before, for three days on my honeymoon with the Ablative Absolute. Now, twenty years later, I revisited those tourist sites I had visited then, replacing the miserable memories I'd retained from that first trip with new ones. When in Rome, I did as the Romans did, plastering over the old, building anew.

Walking among the ruins of the Palatine, I found myself talking to my mother in my head, thinking how much she would have loved seeing these places she must have read about in her many Latin classes. Had she imagined them as she translated? Had she seen photographs? Movies? Perhaps she knew as much Roman history as I did. I could only speculate. My parents never traveled to Europe. My father had no interest, and though my brother Terry had invited Mother to accompany him on one of his many trips to the Continent, she never went with him. I think at that point, in her early sixties, she was afraid to travel, felt unequal to the experience. She was afraid to start anew; instead she allowed the losses of her old life to inter her.

I spent that entire day in ancient Rome and returned too late and too tired to go to class. After all, when Jason introduced me to this or that person, he said, "Ann will be joining us from time to time for the next two weeks." Liberal license from the boss man. There was that handy adjective *liber* again.

I did join the group the next day, the Fourth of July, for a trip by bus to Nemi in the Alban Hills. I sat next to Gina Soter, the teacher of my *juniores* group, the only female among the Paideia teachers, and close to my age. Tall and thin, she was lively, irreverent, and fun. She had studied twice at Reginald's Latin program in the mid-2000s and now ran the residential college at the University of Michigan. She called herself a "cautious zealot" regarding spoken Latin. "Pedagogically, it allows you to do great things, and the ability to use Latin actively has really helped my students learn better."

The name Nemi derives from the Latin *nemus,* or "holy

wood," and overlooks Lake Nemi, a volcanic crater lake. The town itself now stands on what was once the site of the Roman temple of Diana Nemorensis. Diana was the goddess of the hunt, as well as of nature and animals. Though many temples were consecrated to her, the *Nemorensis* (of the grove) was the most famous, and its myth served as the seed for Sir James Frazer's *The Golden Bough.*

For centuries, a sacred oak stood in the center of the grove, which was vigilantly guarded by the *Rex Nemorensis* (King of the Grove and priest of Diana). The *rex* was always an escaped slave, and only another escaped slave was allowed to attempt to break off one of the boughs. If he succeeded, he then engaged the current *rex* in one-on-one combat to death. Whoever prevailed would remain king until another escaped slave who could defeat him came along.

Caligula had dedicated one of his sumptuous ships that plied Lake Nemi to the cult of Diana Nemorensis; the other, a pleasure boat, was tricked out with statues, engravings, baths, sumptuous bronze fittings, and a two-story building. By his era, the succession ritual of the *Rex Nemorensis* had devolved into a forced gladiatorial combat before an audience of Caligula's friends. After Caligula's overthrow, the boats had been sunk in the lake.

We sat on the steps of the Nemi Museum and read and translated passages from Suetonius' *Twelve Caesars.* Then we proceeded to a restaurant overlooking the lake, where a lavish five-course feast, worthy of Caligula, awaited us. After lunch, and plenty of wine, we changed into bathing suits and trooped down to the lake.

As Gina and I walked down the long hill to the lake, a bit worse for wear with wine, we marveled at two of the *seniores* walking in front of us who were reciting lines from Ovid's *Fasti* from our literature booklet about the very site we were approaching.

At the lake, some of the students plunged in at a run, others sat on rocks or towels, some still translated. Gina said, "Okay, you like Ovid, let's read a few lines before we go in. We'll set a good example."

I'd left my literature booklet with my bag at the restaurant, but Gina, a dedicated teacher, hadn't, so she pulled it out and turned to Ovid *Fasti* 3.259.

Quis mihi nunc dicet quare caelestia Martis
arma ferant Salii Mamuriumque canant?
Nympha, mone, nemori stagnoque operata Dianae;
nympha, Numae coniunx, ad tua facta veni.
Vallis Aricinae silva praecinctus opaca
est lacus, antiqua religione sacer.

Before I began to translate, she warned me, "You should know that Mamurium is Mamurius Veturius, who made the shields that hung in the temple of Mars."

Despite that help, I became stuck on *nympha, Numae coniunx, ad tua facta veni.*

"I can't tell if *veni* is the past tense 'I came' or the imperative 'come!' or 'arise!'" I complained. "There's always so much ambiguity."

"Read it again," Gina said. "The first step to disambiguating the syntax is to look again at the word in the larger context of the verse."

And indeed, when I reread it for the fourth time, I realized that it had to be imperative. The imperative, "wait nymph" was in the line before it, and the second *nympha,* at the beginning of the line, gave another clue. "But what about *ad tua facta,*" I asked. "Participles always throw me."

"What do you think it might mean?" Gina asked.

"Well, either 'to your deeds' or 'having been made by you.'"

"What's the meaning of *ad*?" she asked.

"Oh," it suddenly dawned on me that I was confusing *ad,* which meant "to," with *ab,* which meant "by" or "from."

"See," Gina said, "it's not ambiguous, just a very common mistake beginners make. You shouldn't be confusing *ad* with *ab* at this point. You're also making another very common elementary mistake," she added gently, "confusing the personal pronoun with the possessive adjective."

I scoured my mind and finally realized that *tua* was a possessive adjective modifying *facta.* "*O me miseram,*" I wailed. "Four years in and I'm still making elementary mistakes."

"Well," Gina said, "at least you know the difference. Most high school and college students these days can't distinguish between a pronoun and a possessive adjective."

So I figured out it had to be "to your deeds." Maybe I'd never again mix up *ad* and *ab.*

Finally, after more figurative banging of my head, I had it sorted out:

> Now who will tell me why the Salii carry Mars'
> celestial weapons, and sing of their maker.
> Teach me, o nymph, devoted to Diana's lake and
> > woodlands:
> nymph, wife to Numa, arise to your deeds.
> There is a lake, circled by the shady groves of the Ari-
> > cian palisades,
> made sacred by ancient religion.

"Okay," I said, "my brain is fried, let's go jump in the lake."

Together we rose and approached the sacred lake, as Ovid's Arethusa had approached her stream, first dipping in our toes. The water was cold. Then we walked in to our knees. Finally, first Gina, then I, merged with the water. We struck and stroked the water, gliding in a thousand ways, floating through ripples of sunlight.

❧

In honor of the Fourth of July, on the way home we sang "The Star-Spangled Banner" in Latin:

The Star-Spangled Banner

Potestne cerni primo diluculo
Vexillum quod vesperi salutabamus,
Dum stellas clavosque et in proelio
Fluitantes superbe in vallo spectamus?
Atque salvum adhuc interdum subitae
Vexillum noctu ostendebant flammae;
O dic num despectet stellans vexillum
Liberam patriam fortiumque domum.

Then, Jason cued up his computer to the bus's mike. He had downloaded karaoke-style music to pop songs, which had been translated into Latin in our "Songbook." Soon we were all singing along to Journey's *Ne disperetis* ("Don't Stop Believin'"), to Survivor's *Oculus Tigris* ("Eye of the Tiger"), and to my favorite, and wonderfully ironic in the context: Pink Floyd's "Another Brick in the Wall":

Educandi nos non sumus,
Ne coacti credamus,

Sarcasmus ater in conclavi,
Ma . . . gister . . . linque pueros,
Tu omnino later fies hoc in muro
Tu omnino later fies hoc in muro

All in all it's just another brick in the wall.
All in all you're just another brick in the wall.

It was wonderful to hear those students gustily singing that song. They had visited so many bricks in so many walls, ancient, medieval, modern, and postmodern, yet were all too happy to add their own brick, as I was happy to add mine.

❧

I returned to the villa just in time for George's arrival. He'd flown to Venice for four days. He'd never been to Europe on his own and wanted to try it without me serving as translator. How amazed he was at our splendid digs. I gave him a tour: pointing out the various fountains, the "secret garden," the giant dome-shaped topiaries, the villa trees and Roman pines, with their cloud-shaped canopies atop high bare trunks.

Just as darkness fell, we arrived at the stone balustrade on the south portico of the villa, which overlooked all of Rome, known to be one of the most magnificent views of the city. Below us spread thousands of years of history, all mixed together in the gleaming, glowing present. I don't have adjectives superlative enough for our surroundings: Latin sounds more like it felt: *Hortus maximus splendidissimus.* All was beauty, *nulli secundus.*

At the end of the evening, we walked down the long laurel allée, magically lit by the full moon, to the bee fountain and sat in the stone enclosure of its half dome. Above us, a bronze bee harvested from two stone *cornucopiae,* and as we sat silently, the slow drops that fell from the bee's proboscis gradually coalesced into a thin stream, perfectly bisecting the full moon.

I remembered the visualization my healer, Harry Bayne, had given me, those fifteen years before when I'd encountered the box of the void, that void I'd built words around all my life.

"What if the void is not a threat but an opportunity?" he'd asked. And the fathomless black space before me had suddenly transformed into a dance floor. My mother had loved to dance, but she stopped dancing long before she reached my age; she was done, as she said so often. I was not done. I was going to keep on dancing.

CHAPTER 16

There is a pleasure, something so unspeakably thrilling,
in uncovering the other version of our life, that, given a
few days, a few weeks, a few years, this version will be the
only one worth . . . remembering.

—André Aciman, *New York Times,* April 17, 2013

We returned home to high summer in Rhinebeck.
The deer had kindly refrained from eating the
border of zinnias and dahlias I had planted in the
spring, and we were welcomed by a dazzling show. Butterflies
(*papiliones*) were landing on the flowers, darting here and
there, and a hummingbird whizzed overhead as we were
unpacking the luggage from the car. Why shouldn't I be completely happy in such a paradise?

The day after our arrival, a package arrived from my brother
Terry. It contained a newspaper clipping in a plastic sleeve and
a silver box. The clipping was dated February 25, 1938, and its
headline read "Broad Ripple Enters Latin Contest," and
below it a photograph. There, in the middle of a triangle
formed by six students, sits my mother, the only one of the
students shown down to the knees, the only one smiling. She's
far and away the prettiest of the four girls who surround her

like bridesmaids. The lone boy, looking alarmingly serious, looms above her.

The silver box contained a small gold pendant in the shape of a Roman galley, with *Virgil* embossed on its sail. It was the Latin medal Mother had won at the statewide Indiana contest. I'd never seen it before.

After Mother's death, I'd stayed with my father for a week. Three days before I was due to leave, I asked him if there was anything I could do for him. He told me he'd like me to pack up Mother's clothes; he didn't think he could bear to do that. I spent four hours in a white heat taking her clothes off hangers and out of drawers, folding them up and boxing them. I listened to the same songs over and over: Tracy Chapman singing "Fast Car" and "She's Got Her Ticket."

I worked like an automaton, rarely stopping to associate memories with the dresses and blouses I was carelessly folding and dropping in the box, in a hurry as usual. I saved a few things I thought my siblings might want, and the next day took the boxes to Goodwill; eight of them, laid end to end, would roughly be the size of a casket. I saved one cashmere sweater she had always prized for myself, along with her diamond earrings and her jewelry box stuffed with costume jewelry. I was angry with her that day I boxed her up and discarded her; angry that she had drunk herself out of this life. Why hadn't she found anything to be but mother and wife, why had she given in, plunged into the void?

Now my benevolent Terry has given me her Latin medal. I have strung the pendant on a gold chain that has languished in her old jewelry box for years. I wear it around my neck. When I feel anxious and feel my engine revving, I touch the medal. I think my mother can calm me. She wasn't one to get rattled and anxious, as I do. She was sad and empty. The part of me that is her fills the emptiness with words. If she were alive, she would certainly recognize herself in me now. I have changed my own past and reclaimed hers. She sails this sea with me.

finis

ACKNOWLEDGMENTS

I owe gratitude to many individuals and institutions that were essential to the writing of this book.

My brilliant daughter, Sophie Withers, showed me how scholarship and perseverance can change a life.

Abigail Thomas convinced me that I could and should write, and gave me essential support and encouragement all along the way.

Curtis Dozier, *summus magister* and *bonus amicus,* allowed me to embark on this journey. Without him, this book, and my life, would be much less interesting.

Steve Magnuson has been the best of friends. His intelligence, honesty, and willingness to spend hours discussing things Latin and literary with me have made this book, and me, our best selves.

I was blessed with brilliant teachers: Matthew Wright, J. Bert Lott, Robert Brown, Benjamin Stevens, Daniel Gallagher, Gina Soter, and Charlie McNamara.

Stephen Haff, the bodhisattva of Still Waters in the Storm, keeps Latin alive in a most creative and beautiful manner, and allowed me to teach for the first time.

Jason Pedicone of the Paideia Institute kindly welcomed me into his thriving community, which is a beacon of hope for the study of Latin and Greek.

Vassar College and Bard College were superlative places to study. Both maintain an admirable dedication to the classics. The American Academy in Rome allowed me to enjoy a splendid accommodation during my visit to Rome.

For ideas, encouragement, and help of many varieties, I am indebted to Judy Lee Hartnett, Lilla Lyon, Patrick McGrath, Elisa Petrini, Jan Heller Levi, Nancy Mujo Baker, Margaret Thornton, Anna Adresian, Michael Fontaine, George Hodgman, Sam Swope, Jane Isay, Stephanie Gangi, and Peter Trachtenberg.

I thank my wizardly agent, Meg Ruley, and everyone at the Jane Rotrosen Agency for their savvy, enthusiasm, and care. My supersmart editor, Paul Slovak, was exacting and subtle, truly an editor's editor.

Finally, I am grateful to George Vengrin, *coniunx optimus,* without whom I would have no romance.